INSIDE
CHARLIE'S
CHOCOLATE
FACTORY

INSIDE CHARLIE'S CHOCOLATE FACTORY

The Complete Story of Willy Wonka,
the Golden Ticket, and
ROALD DAHL'S
Most Famous Creation

LUCY MANGAN

PUFFIN BOOKS
An Imprint of Penguin Group (USA)

PUFFIN BOOKS

Published by the Penguin Group

Penguin Group (USA) LLC

375 Hudson Street

New York, New York 10014

USA | Canada | UK | Ireland | Australia
New Zealand | India | South Africa | China

penguin.com
A Penguin Random House Company

Published simultaneously in Great Britain by Penguin Books and in the United States by Puffin Books, an imprint of Penguin Young Readers Group, 2014

LIBRARY OF CONGRESS CATALOGING-IN-PUBLICATION DATA
Mangan, Lucy.
Inside Charlie's Chocolate Factory : the Complete Story of Willy Wonka, the Golden Ticket, and Roald Dahl's Most Famous Creation / by Lucy Mangan.
p. cm.
Includes bibliographical references and index.
ISBN 978-0-14-751348-9 (pbk.)
[1. Dahl, Roald. *Charlie and the Chocolate Factory*—Juvenile literature. 2. Dahl, Roald—Film and video adaptations—Juvenile literature. 3. Children's stories, English—History and criticism—Juvenile literature.]
I. Title.
PR6054.A35Z737 2014
823'.914—dc23
2014007560

Designed by Mandy Norman
Picture research by Raffaella Morini
Printed in China

10 9 8 7 6 5 4 3 2 1

CONTENTS

THE RED CHOCOLATE BOX

I called him Mold, because when I was a toddler my baby tongue couldn't get to grips with the Norwegian pronunciation of his name, 'Roo-al' (regal, long stretched *Roo, al* like the end of mall, silent *D*), and instead Mold he was, ever after.

Sophie Dahl, aged three.

At his table, I was raised on a steady diet of good food and enchantment. A meal was never just a meal; it was a recipe from a prince in Dar es Salaam, rescued from the jaws of a hungry python at the crucial moment by my grandfather. In this story, and its variants, Mold was always the blue-eyed interloper, diverting the disasters he stumbled upon. So grateful was the fictitious prince, he gave the lanky Englishman his treasured recipe for crab-stuffed baked potatoes. (Or toast with bacon and marmalade, or whatever else happened to be on the menu in rainy Buckinghamshire that day.)

He had many accoutrements of magic, Mold, like a proper magician should: amaretto biscuits whose wrapping paper you lit, which shot up into the sky like titchy hot-air balloons, falling back to earth in a wispy question mark of ash; a miniature steam train that huffed and puffed round the dining room table; a house dotted with Witch Balls, ancient, mirrored spheres that hung from a window, confronting any witch so bold as to come knocking with her own hideous reflection so she'd flee. Mold was famous among his children, and later on me, for writing our names in the grass with weed killer, while we slept.

'The fairies have been,' he'd say over breakfast, in a voice that crackled and sparked, like the beginnings of a bonfire.

There was nothing more magical, though, than the Red Tupperware Box that appeared at the end of a meal, heralding the most important and longed-for bit.

The Red Tupperware was a medium-sized, rectangular box of function. The box itself was almost irrelevant, and it could have been blue, green or see-through. Its postbox redness, though, lent an air of jaunty dissolution to the proceedings and ultimately became part of its own myth.

If you had been good at lunch or dinner, not too much of a bore, eaten things proffered without a fuss, you could collect the fabled box from its home in the kitchen and bring it to the table, while the grown-ups were having their coffee.

The Red Box contained chocolate. Lots of chocolate, in child-sized appealing bars, nothing fancy, but always compelling. And it was here, over this staunch bit of plastic, that Mold and I did a great deal of communing.

We both LOVED chocolate. Our taste in the stuff was similar. Cadbury's Flake, Aero, Curly Wurly, Crunchie, KitKat and the Dime bar, a Scandinavian crunchy concoction that Mold delivered to me with great ceremony after a book tour in Sweden. Maltesers, Rolo, Fruit and Nut; a mutual horror of the Creme Egg. We were partners in a quest for the ultimate bite (light, airy, possibly featuring almonds). His knowledge of chocolate was encyclopedic. He could recall specific dates and years of invention with the glee of a patriotic child recalling the kings and queens of his country. Even his Jack Russell, Chopper, ate chocolate (four Smarties, served after lunch and dinner, daily).

Mold grew up fatherless in Wales, in an era before chocolate was readily available. Sweet shops peppered his boyhood and boyhood writing: lemon sherbets, bootlaces, gobstoppers and toffees, hard-boiled sweets served by boot-faced proprietors. Chocolate was later: the stuff of dreams, exotic and faraway.

And so, for the grown-up Mold, Willy Wonka and his factory were to embody the chocolate dream, Charlie Bucket to play the moral compass beating at its heart. *Charlie and the Chocolate Factory* was written fifty years ago, but it remains utterly timeless and infused with a child-like magic that only a landscape of chocolate rivers and everlasting gobstoppers can conjure. For each and every one of us, there remains a powerful, Proustian memory of that first-ever something sweet, and, for so many of us, that was made flesh by the story of Charlie Bucket and his Golden Ticket.

A journalist asked Mold before he died, how he liked his chocolate. He answered thus: 'For the record, I am not overly fond of chocolate-flavoured foods such as chocolate cake and chocolate ice cream. I prefer my chocolate straight.'

So do I.

Happy 50th Birthday, Charlie.

Sophie Dahl

WELCOME TO THE FACTORY

It's not quite the first time I've had reason to be thankful for my parents', um . . . well, let's call them 'eccentricities' regarding my upbringing, but I have not felt quite such a fervent gratitude before.

I wasn't allowed many sweets or chocolate as a child. I could take a decorous few at parties, or one chocolate digestive or a sucky-sweet after dinner when I got older, and my beloved grandma gave me a Cadbury's Buttons egg at Easter. I used to make it last for weeks – buttons first, then shell. *Charlie and the Chocolate Factory* spoke to me as no other book before or since has done. I knew that feeling of watching other children cramming chocolate down their throats in front of me (yes, it was indeed pure torture) and the unspeakable elation of occasionally getting my own hands on the stuff and letting the creamy sweetness flood my mouth and fill my senses.

The book transported me with other delights. The sense of recklessness, of adventure, of dreams tethered just close enough to reality to allow you to think that they might honestly one day come true. It was, I think, the first 'proper' book I ever read – mostly words, not pictures (like *Where the Wild Things Are*), and telling just one story (not like Teddy Robinson, who had lots of little ones) that gathered you up, whizzed you along at a glorious, dizzying pace and tipped you out, dazed, breathless but – crucially – not confused at the end. At which point, all you had to do was turn back to the first page and start again, this time with the joy of anticipation infusing it all with an extra, even more mouth-watering savour.

This book is written for all those who loved *Charlie and the Chocolate Factory* when they were young, and those who love it now. It's for anyone who wants to know a bit more about how it came to be, how it managed to permeate readers' worlds and the world at large, and how it has endured so happily for fifty years – and counting.

It's been a whipple-scrumptious fudgemallow delight to do. I hope you have half as much fun reading it as I did writing it.

Welcome to the factory.

Lucy Mangan

SUGAR-COATED PENCILS
Writing the Book

CLOCKWISE FROM ABOVE LEFT:
Charlie and the Chocolate Factory has been translated into fifty-five languages, including: Swedish (Tidens Forlag, 2007); Georgian (Bakur Sulakauri Publishing, 2010); Tamil (Vikatan, 2008); French (Gallimard Jeunesse, 1978); and Arabic (Samir Éditeur, 2011).

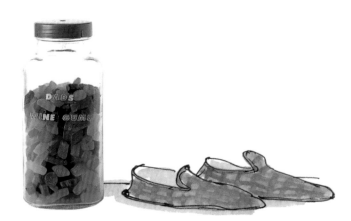

Introduction

In 1960 Roald Dahl was living in America with his wife, the film star Patricia Neal, their two daughters, Olivia and Tessa, and their newborn son, Theo. To entertain the children, Roald Dahl would make up stories. One of them was about a lonely boy who lived in a town that was also home to an extraordinary chocolate factory. 'Having read my children all the available books and come across some really crummy ones,' he said later, 'I thought – why not try to write a children's book?'

So began the gestation of the story that would lead to one of Roald Dahl's best-known, bestselling, best-loved creations, *Charlie and the Chocolate Factory*.

Most of us, when we read as children, imagine vaguely (if we imagine the author at all) that he or she simply sat down one day and wrote seamlessly, line after line, page after page, exactly the book we were reading – as if transcribing something already fully realized in his or her head. Today's children in English schools – well versed in the national-curriculum directive to plan, draft and edit their writing – are probably less naive, but it's still tempting to imagine that, to the best writers, stories all come easily.

Of course, with very rare exceptions, the creative process isn't that kind. It is almost never a matter of simply putting thoughts on to paper,

PREVIOUS SPREAD:
Roald Dahl and his dog
Chopper getting his daily treat
(1988). (Illustrations by
Quentin Blake.)

ABOVE:
Photograph of Roald's jar of
wine gums, and his slippers
illustrated by Quentin Blake.

Romanian edition (Editura Arthur, 2012).

Ukrainian edition (A-Ba-Ba-Ha-La-Ma-Ha Publishers, 2005).

typing it up and handing it in. Writers draft and redraft, paring down parts of their original version, building up others, adding and subtracting characters, plotlines, chapters, paragraphs and generally doing whatever is necessary to narrow the distance between what exists in the mind's eye and what turns up on the page.

For all its casual, effortless-looking brilliance, Roald Dahl took his writing seriously and worked hard at it. The plot of a short story – which was the form of writing that first made him famous – could take him weeks to perfect. His first book for children, *James and the Giant Peach* (published in 1961), took two years to write. *Charlie*, however, took even longer to bring to fruition because during its writing Roald suffered two of the greatest blows of his life.

The first came on 5 December 1960, a few months after Roald had sent a first draft of the story, then titled 'Charlie's Chocolate Boy', to his US literary agent, Mike Watkins.

The Dahls' nanny was pushing their baby, Theo, in his pram through New York City as she brought three-year-old Tessa home from her nursery school for lunch. As they crossed the road at the corner of 85th Street and Madison Avenue, a taxi hit the pram. The pram was thrown into the side of a bus and crushed. Theo was terribly, terribly injured and at first it looked to the doctors as if he would not survive. He did, but developed hydrocephalus (when spinal fluid accumulates around the brain, putting damaging pressure on it) and had to undergo repeated operations to insert a shunt into his head to drain the fluid away. It had to be done again and again because the shunt's valve kept clogging, causing Theo to develop a fever and become temporarily blind each time. Shortly after the family returned to England in May 1961, Theo suffered another relapse.

While the doctors were doing everything they could for Theo, Roald set himself to investigating whether there was

Inside Charlie's Chocolate Factory

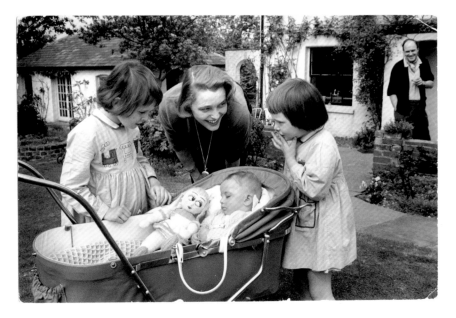

any better shunt available. When he found there wasn't – many children with Theo's type of injuries were having to undergo the same multiple surgeries – Roald began discussing the matter with Theo's neurosurgeon, Kenneth Till, mining every ounce of Till's expert understanding of the problem. Roald then took the problem to his friend Stanley Wade. Wade was an engineer whose hobby was making miniature engines for toy aeroplanes and who ran a factory in High Wycombe, Buckinghamshire, which produced precision hydraulic pumps.

Together, and almost unbelievably, the three men invented and produced a new and better valve. In June 1962 the first Wade–Dahl–Till valve was inserted into the head of a patient in Great Ormond Street Hospital for Sick Children in London. It worked beautifully. Eighteen months later, it was on the market, and at less than a third of the cost of its rival. It happened so swiftly and cost so little because the three men had agreed from the beginning never to accept any profit from it. It was exported all over the world and – although Theo was well enough not to need it by the time his father's invention was ready – it was used to treat thousands of children before it was superseded by newer technology.

Roald Dahl dedicated *Charlie and the Chocolate Factory* to his son. 'I don't remember when I first opened the book and saw my name in it,' says Theo, who now lives in Florida with his wife and daughter. 'But I always found Charlie unwrapping his Golden Ticket the best part. I love the book. It was a beautiful book to have dedicated to me.'

In January 1962, Sheila St Lawrence, who'd worked with Mike Watkins, wrote to Roald Dahl, evidently in response to a letter from him saying that he was suffering from writer's block: 'It is wonderful news that Theo is doing so well. I suppose that Pat and you rarely have a calm and unworried moment. "Charlie's Chocolate Boy" will just have to come along in his own good time when you're in the mood for him.'

By the autumn of 1962, relief and happiness at Theo's recovery seemed to have freed Roald enough to produce a second draft of 'Charlie's Chocolate Boy' – now renamed *Charlie and the Chocolate Factory* – in which he had enough confidence to send it to his publisher, Knopf. He had just received an enthusiastic letter about it from Virginie Fowler, Knopf's editor of children's books, when a second and even crueller blow struck the family.

Olivia and Tessa arrived home from school with a note warning parents about a measles outbreak. Wholesale vaccination against the disease did not exist then – trials were being held, and it would be

Inside Charlie's Chocolate Factory

introduced in the US just a year later and in the UK in 1968 – and while a special dose was obtained for the still terribly fragile Theo, it could not be made available for anyone else.

Seven-year-old Olivia caught the bug and was put to bed. She slept for twenty-four hours and her mother called the doctor, who came and went without notable alarm. Roald tried to entertain her by making little animals out of coloured pipe cleaners, but she remained drowsy and eventually fell asleep again. When the doctor returned, he realized she had slipped into a coma and called an ambulance. Olivia was taken to hospital and died there that night.

It is perhaps both impossible and unwise to try to describe the depths of anyone's grief at losing a child. Recalling it twenty years later in her autobiography, Patricia Neal still struggled to articulate her own grief, and says simply of her husband that he 'all but lost his mind'.

Writing is a solitary and inward-looking profession, which was unhelpful in such a situation as Roald's at that time. In a letter to his publishers six months later Roald wrote, 'I feel right now as though I'll never in my life do any more! I simply cannot seem to get started again.'

Eventually, however, the need – both financial and personal – to work reasserted itself and another draft of *Charlie* took shape. And another. And another.

Mr. Wonka proudly. "And all you have to do is to pop one of those little warming-candies into your mouth and suck it, and if you're feeling cold or shivery, it'll warm you up all over. Why, you can actually stand out in the snow on a freezing day with no clothes on at all, and just so long as you are sucking one of these tiny sweets, then you'll feel warm as toast."

"It's crazy," said another father.

"It's true," said Mr. Wonka. "And I'd gladly give one to each of you right now to try for yourselves — except that it would only make you hotter than ever on such a very hot day as this."

"It's all baloney!" said a boy called Clarence Crump.

"Baloney is right!" said a second boy whose name was Bertie Upside. "You could eat a <u>sackful</u> of that junk and you wouldn't feel any hotter!"

"Why don't we prove it?" cried a third boy called Terrence Roper. Whereupon, all three of them ran forward to the heap of little red warming-candies and started cramming handfuls of them into their mouths as fast as they could.

"Foolish boys," murmured Mr. Wonka.

"It's just as I said!" shouted Clarence

Manuscript page from the earliest existing draft of 'Charlie's Chocolate Boy' (*c.* 1961).

The Manuscripts

Altogether, there are five drafts of *Charlie and the Chocolate Factory* in existence. An earlier one is lost, but according to Roald, recalling it years later:

> *The very first time I did it, I got everything wrong. I wrote a story about a little boy who was going round a chocolate factory and he accidentally fell into a big tub of melted chocolate and got sucked unto the machine that made chocolate figures and he couldn't get out. It was a splendid big chocolate figure, a chocolate boy the same size as him. And it was Easter time, and the figure was put in a shop window, and at the end a lady came in and bought it as an Easter present for her little girl and carried it home. On Easter Day, the little girl opened the box with her present in it and took it out, and then she decided to eat some of it. She would start with the head, she thought. So she broke off the nose and when she saw a real human nose sticking out underneath and two bright human eyes staring at her through the eye-holes in the chocolate she got a nasty shock. And so it went on.*

The only other thing we can surmise about that very first version – thanks to one uncorrected hangover in the subsequent draft – is that Willy Wonka originally went by the slightly less memorable title of Mr Ritchie. This following draft still exists in all its glory. It is made up of typed pages from the now-lost first version, with some typed sections taped on to handwritten pages. However, a substantial amount is written in longhand, using – as Roald did for the drafts of all his books – a Dixon Ticonderoga pencil on yellow legal pads. They were both commonplace in the US, where he had first found fame as a writer and where he was living when he began writing *Charlie*, but when he returned to live in England a few years later he had to have them sent over specially.

It was this second draft, neatly typed by his secretary, that had arrived on Mike Watkins's desk in 1960 just before Theo suffered his accident.

'Charlie's Chocolate Boy' told the story of an eccentric (though not nearly as eccentric as he was to become) chocolate-maker called Willy Wonka who, having been forced to abandon his open-door policy for visitors to his factory because of the riots caused by thousands of people struggling to get in every day, sends out ten Golden Tickets hidden in his chocolate bars every week. Charlie Bucket is a poor, malnourished child (thanks to what was at this stage a potato-only rather than cabbage diet) who in this version doesn't even get a birthday bar of chocolate every year but becomes one of that week's lucky ten when he finds a coin in the gutter, buys a Wonka Whipped Cream Marshmallow Delight and discovers a Golden Ticket inside.

His nine companions are: Augustus Pottle and Miranda Grope (who both end up in the chocolate river and, shortly thereafter, get sucked up two glass pipes to the Chocolate Caramel and Peanut Brittle Rooms respectively); Wilbur Rice and Tommy Troutbeck (who end up in the Pounding and Cutting Room after playing havoc with mining operations on the vanilla-fudge mountain); Violet Strabismus (née Glockenberry, before Roald hit upon the medical term for a squint, who turns purple after chowing down on the three-course gum that is still in the experimental phase of development); Clarence Crump, Bertie Upside, Trevor Roper (who all overheat after ingesting an unwise number of Warming Candies); and finally Elvira Entwhistle, brat of brats, who gets pitched down the rubbish chute by – yes! – the trained squirrels in the Nut Room.

After that, Charlie is treated to a look at the Easter Egg room, which contains chocolate eggs 'the size of automobiles', life-sized chocolate animals and row upon row of chocolate men, women, boys, girls and babies. Charlie cannot resist trying one of the boy-moulds for size and – before you can say 'Hang on, this is nothing like the book!' – he is encased in a thick, unbreakable shell of chocolate and sent to Mr Wonka's house as an Easter present for his son.

While Charlie's there, he manages to foil a robbery, and as a reward Mr Wonka gives him his own chocolate shop, nine storeys high. The tale ends with Charlie taking his friends there after school: '"It's my shop," he tells them. "Just help yourselves." And they do.'

Reading 'Charlie's Chocolate Boy' is a very enjoyable but

Inside Charlie's Chocolate Factory

CHAPTER ONE
WONKA'S FACTORY

CHARLIE'S CHOCOLATE BOY

THE LARGEST CHOCOLATE FACTORY IN THE WORLD IS OWNED BY A
MAN CALLED MR. WILLY WONKA. IT IS A SIMPLY ENORMOUS FACTORY.
IT IS ALSO A VERY FINE ONE, AND IF YOU LOOK NOW, YOU CAN SEE
MR. WONKA QUITE EASILY. HE IS THE ONE STANDING PROUDLY JUST
OUTSIDE THE MAIN GATES WITH A SILK HAT ON HIS HEAD AND A CANE
IN ONE HAND.

with a beard who is

MR. WONKA IS EXTRAORDINARILY CLEVER. HE HAS HIMSELF
INVENTED MORE THAN TWO HUNDRED NEW KINDS OF CANDY-BAR, EACH WITH
A DIFFERENT CENTRE, EACH OF THEM SOMEHOW SWEETER AND CREAMIER
AND MORE EXCITING THAN ANYTHING ~~THAN ANYTHING~~ THAT THE OTHER
CHOCOLATE FACTORIES CAN MAKE.

MR. WONKA HAS ALSO DISCOVERED A WAY OF MAKING A CHOCOLATE
ICE-CREAM SO THAT IT STAYS COLD FOR HOURS AND HOURS WITHOUT BEING
IN THE ICEBOX. YOU CAN EVEN LEAVE IT LYING IN THE ~~SNOW~~ *sun* ALL
MORNING ON A HOT DAY AND IT WON'T GO RUNNY. MR. WONKA CAN MAKE
MARSHMALLOWS THAT TASTE OF VIOLETS, AND RICH CARAMELS THAT CHANGE
COLOUR EVERY TEN SECONDS AS YOU SUCK THEM, AND LITTLE FEATHERY
SWEETS THAT MELT AWAY DELICIOUSLY THE MOMENT YOU PUT THEM BETWEEN
YOUR LIPS. HE CAN MAKE CHEWING-GUM THAT NEVER LOSES ITS TASTE,
AND CANDY BALLOONS THAT YOU CAN BLOW UP TO ENORMOUS SIZES BEFORE
YOU POP THEM WITH A PIN AND GOBBLE THEM UP. AND BY A MOST
SECRET METHOD, HE CAN MAKE LOVELY BLUE BIRDS' EGGS WITH BLACK SPOTS
ON THEM, AND WHEN YOU PUT ONE OF THESE IN YOUR MOUTH IT GRADUALLY
GETS SMALLER AND SMALLER UNTIL SUDDENLY THERE IS NOTHING LEFT EXCEPT
A TINY LITTLE PINK SUGARY *baby-* BIRD SITTING ON THE TIP OF YOUR TONGUE. //

discombobulating experience – full of familiar landmarks, but in an unfamiliar country. The river's there, but it's just in a room. There's no meadow full of minty grass and sugar buttercups. And there's no waterfall. What's Wonka's factory without a waterfall? And wait – Wonka has a wife and child? A home? What are these uniformed (brown and gold, 'the Wonka colours') adult workers doing everywhere? Where are the Oompa-Loompas? And where, oh where, is my favourite bit – the square sweets that look round? (I was thirteen – five years older than when I'd actually read the book – when it suddenly dawned on me, in the middle of a maths class, what that meant. I didn't know whether to punch the air in triumph or bang my head on the desk in despair.)

Then there are the ghosts – or, perhaps more accurately, the spirits – of favourites yet to come. Prince Pondicherry's palace is not in the first draft, but it has a definite precursor in the ten-room mansion Mr Wonka builds for 'a very rich man' who is thwarted by the sun's tendency to melt his chosen building material until Mr Wonka invents a new, heat-resistant kind (itself a reminder of the non-melting ice cream to come). And there are the whispering, disembodied voices that can be heard singing about the children's fates as they (or their distraught parents) are ferried away – whose verses will later be put into the mouths of a new workforce: the Whipple-Scrumpets, as the Oompa-Loompas are known at first.

Two of Roald Dahl's most distinguishing features – his authorial/narrative confidence and his companionable tone that speaks unusually and thrillingly directly to the child reader – are there from the very first draft. 'Charlie's Chocolate Boy' begins: 'The largest chocolate factory in the world is owned by a man called Mr Willy Wonka. It is a simply enormous factory. It is also a very fine one, and if you look now, you can see Mr Wonka quite easily. He is the one with a beard who is

OPPOSITE: A page from a later draft, showing the last-minute change from 'Whipple-Scrumpet' to 'Oompa-Loompa' in Roald's own hand (*c*. autumn, 1963).

Inside Charlie's Chocolate Factory

CHAPTER 20

THE INVENTING ROOM - EVERLASTING GOBSTOPPERS
AND HAIR-TOFFEE

Oompa-Loompas   1

When Mr Wonka shouted "Stop the boat!", the ~~Whipple-Scrumpets~~ —
jammed their oars into the river and backed water furiously. The
boat stopped.

    Oompa-Loompas   4
The ~~Whipple-Scrumpets~~ guided the boat alongside the red door.
On the door it said, INVENTING ROOM - PRIVATE - KEEP OUT.
Mr Wonka took a key from his pocket and leaned over the side of
the boat and put the key in the keyhole.

"This is the most important room in the entire factory!" he
said. "All my most secret new inventions are cooking and
simmering in here! Old Pickelgruber would give his front teeth
to be allowed inside just for three minutes! So would Prodnose
and Slugworth and all the other rotten chocolate makers! But
now listen to me! I want no messing about when you go in! No
touching, no meddling, and no tasting! Is that agreed?"

"Yes, yes!" the children cried. "We won't touch a thing!"

"Up to now," Mr Wonka said, "nobody else, not even a ~   — 16
Oompa-Loompa
~~Whipple-Scrumpet~~, has ever been allowed in here!" He opened the — 7
door and stepped out of the boat into the room. The four
children and their parents all scrambled after him.

"Don't touch!" shouted Mr Wonka. "Don't knock anything
over!"

22nd October, 1971

Willy Wonka Esq.,
Blue Hill,
Nebraska 68930,
U. S. A.

Dear Mr. Willy Wonka,

I was delighted to get your letter and the press
clipping with a picture of you. First of all, you and
your friends really must believe me when I say that I picked
your name out of the air. When I was a small boy my elder
brother use to make for me a kind of boomerang and he always
called it Skilly Wonka. When I was writing my book and
searching for a name I remembered this and by changing two
letters only I arrived at Willy Wonka. This is the absolute
truth, although I have so far told it to no-one but you.

I will try to think up some kind of an object for
you to stick on your mail van but I think this is going to
defeat me because the thing has to be weather proof does it
not? Write and let me know if you would not prefer to have
an autographed copy of "Charlie and the Chocolate Factory".
I would be very happy to send you one.

Yours sincerely,

Roald Dahl.

standing proudly just outside the main gates with a silk hat on his head
and a cane in one hand.' It's a straight line from there to the opening of
Charlie and the Chocolate Factory as we know it, with the narrator
breaking with the usual convention in children's (and indeed adult)
fiction to make his presence felt by introducing his characters
personally to the reader – grandparents, parents and of course: 'This is
Charlie. How d'you do? And how d'you do? And how d'you do again?
He is pleased to meet you.'

And there you are, right in the middle of things, secure in the
knowledge that you are in good hands but unable to predict where they
are going to take you. What other rules might be broken along the way?
The maverick Roald Dahl has you, in short, right where he wants you.

That said, what is noticeable in the first draft is a general sense of
unripeness, of an imagination not yet quite off the leash – even

Inside Charlie's Chocolate Factory

occasional overt caution. This first Wonka, for example, assures Charlie that the melted chocolate in the river is not too hot to dip his finger into, tells Mrs Pottle that Augustus will be quite all right after a bath and ensures that Violet gets taken to the factory hospital to be sorted out. Perhaps Roald still felt too much like the father who had been telling the story to his children to leave his sense of paternal responsibility behind completely. Perhaps, despite his success with his first children's book, *James and the Giant Peach*, which had earned almost universally enthusiastic reviews with steady if not spectacular sales since its publication, he hadn't yet quite realized just how far his audience would be willing to go with him on fantastical adventures.

Still, even here you can already sense what we think of now as the true Roald Dahl, moving underneath the story like a shark – and occasionally breaking the surface to show his grinning teeth. When Tommy heads off to the Pounding and Cutting Room, for example, where 'a whole lot of knives come down and go chop, chop, chop, cutting it up into neat little squares', his loving mother bellows in dismay, 'No boy of mine is going to be put in shop windows and sold as vanilla fudge! We've spent far too much on his education already!' Mr Wonka assures her that there is a large wire strainer there to catch children before they fall into the machine. 'It always catches them. At least, it always has up to now.'

Over the next few drafts, you can see the story beginning to take flight. The large cast of characters is whittled down from ten to five, with new ones being introduced and discarded in between, and the remaining ones renamed. We bid farewell to Miranda Mary Piker. Marvin Prune is pruned. Bertie Upside, Trevor Roper, Crump – gone, gone, gone (their Warming Candies living on, perhaps, as the hot ice cream that 'warms you up no end in freezing weather' and the hot ice cubes that 'make hot drinks hotter'). Wilbur Rice and Tommy Troutbeck get left on the Pounding and Cutting Room floor. The scene of their demise, the fudge mountain, becomes just a vision in the distance glimpsed by Charlie as he hurtles past in the Great Glass Elevator on his way up and out of the factory. Augustus Pottle becomes Gloop, Elvira Entwhistle becomes Veruca Salt, Violet Strabismus changes surname to Beauregarde, and new boy Mike Teavee arrives.

NEXT SPREAD (LEFT):
Roald Dahl's sketches of the children in the book, including Miranda Mary Piker, the last character to be cut.

NEXT SPREAD (RIGHT):
The Oompa-Loompas' song about Miranda Mary Piker, handwritten by Roald.

4th draft.

R. leave spaces for small drawings

THERE ARE SIX CHILDREN IN THIS BOOK:

AUGUSTUS GLOOP — A greedy boy

MIRANDA MARY PIKER — A girl who is allowed
To do anything she likes.

VERUCA SALT — A girl who is allowed
To have anything she wants.

VIOLET BEAUREGARDE — A girl who chews
Gum all day long.

MIKE TEAVEE — A boy who is crazy
about Television.

And the child we like best of all

CHARLIE BUCKET

MIRANDA MARY PIKER
IS MADE INTO PEANUT-BRITTLE

(This character was deleted from the final version
of Charlie and the Chocolate Factory)

Oh, Miranda Mary Piker,
How could anybody like her,
Such a rude and disobedient little kid,
So we said why don't we fix her
In the Peanut-Brittle Mixer
Then we're sure to like her better than we did.
Soon this girl who was so vicious
Will have gotten quite delicious
And her parents will have surely understood
That instead of saying "Miranda,
"Oh, the beast we cannot stand her!"
They'll be saying, "Oh, how tasty and how good!"

Charlie himself moves to centre stage and becomes the small, stalwart foil to Willy Wonka's increasingly appealing and mercurial inventor. Grandpa Joe gets out of bed and takes his rightful place at Charlie's side. And the Oompa-Loompas arrive! From Africa originally, rather than Loompaland, a decision that – as we shall see – would later cause Roald some difficulty and which he would change for a new edition a few years later, but come they do and suddenly everything starts to look a lot more – well, *Charlie and the Chocolate Factory*ish. Especially when, after dropping the whole chocolate-boy-and-burglary plot, Roald renames his story *Charlie and the Chocolate Factory*.

Situations comic and frightening are pushed to the limit and every possibility is exploited to the full. Out goes the Easter-egg production line, in comes a bigger, better Inventing Room, full of Everlasting

Inside Charlie's Chocolate Factory

Gobstoppers and Hair Toffee and a gum machine that has evolved from a modest table-top device to the magnificent Heath Robinsonesque contraption we now know – a tangle of multicoloured glass tubes sprouting out of a tower of metal – dedicated to the pursuit of the perfect stick of tomato-soup-roast-dinner-and-blueberry-pie-and-cream-flavoured gum. Instead of Mr Wonka assuring Mr and Mrs Entwhistle (the parents of Veruca Salt's predecessor, Elvira) that their child is likely to get stuck in the rubbish chute and come to no harm, he now encourages them to go and look down the hole to see if she is there – whereupon, of course, the squirrels boot them head-first down after her. The chocolate river gets its waterfall, its meadow and a boiled-sweet boat to cruise along it. Violet no longer merely turns blue; she swells up like a blueberry and has to be rolled to the Juicing Room. And Charlie, of course, morphs from burglar-catcher into Willy Wonka's heir apparent. Even the corridors are transformed: no longer ordinary walkways but hung with tantalizing signs suggesting an infinity of

fantastical delights – EATABLE MARSHMALLOW PILLOWS, LICKABLE WALLPAPER FOR NURSERIES, FIZZY LIFTING DRINKS. Like the gum machine, the whole thing now vibrates and bubbles with life and colour. From a handful of innocuous ingredients and some energetic experimentation, Roald Dahl's imagination produces a magnificent three-course meal.

The last few drafts show Roald giving some last-minute polishes and tweaks to his creation – only in the final one, for example, does Charlie's winning purchase become the Whipple-scrumptious Fudgemallow Delight of legend – and there it is, all ready for publication in June 1964.

The first US edition of
*Charlie and the
Chocolate Factory.*
(Knopf, 1964).

Inside Charlie's Chocolate Factory

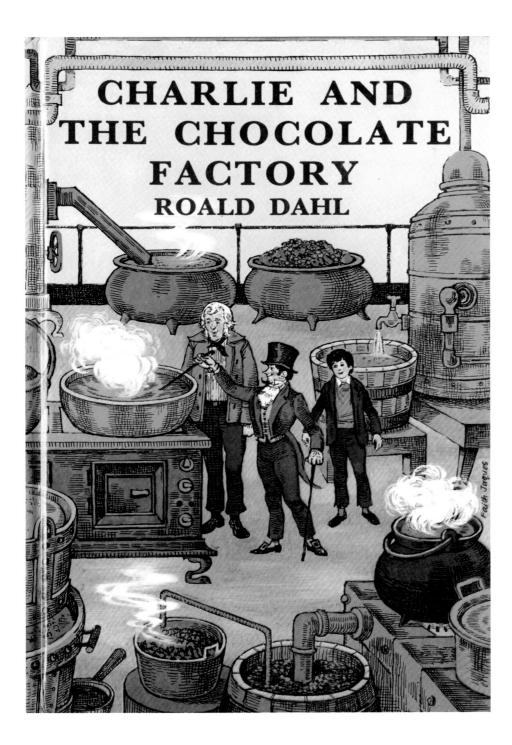

The first UK edition of *Charlie and the Chocolate Factory*, illustrated by Faith Jaques (Allen & Unwin, 1967).

JAMES AND
THE GIANT PEACH
by ROALD DAHL

illustrated by NANCY EKHOLM BURKERT

First US edition of *James and the Giant Peach* (Knopf, 1961).

Inside Charlie's Chocolate Factory

The Story Behind the Story

Roald Dahl was greatly helped in his reworking of 'Charlie's Chocolate Boy', as he had been during the writing of *James and the Giant Peach*, by his former agent Sheila St Lawrence, whose instincts and editorial talents he much admired and trusted. She had in fact been the first person to suggest (several years earlier) that Roald would be a good writer of children's fiction. Although she had by 1960 given up her career and gone to live in Ireland with her husband and three children, Roald asked Mike Watkins to forward her the draft that Roald had sent in December 1960 before Theo's accident and to solicit her advice. St Lawrence sent him back a letter that began: 'I've read "Charlie's Chocolate Boy"; re-read it to the children, and then gone over it again myself . . . I can't tell you how excited I was with the idea of the story. It's marvellous.' She went on to make a variety of suggestions both large (or potentially large – 'I would like to see the assistants either chocolate mechanical boys or animals or something more surprising than they are') and small ('Might it be amusing to have Augustus stick in the pipe for a fleeting moment, like a blob of ice cream in a straw and then pop forward as he is dislodged?'), along with some other extra-textual practical considerations. For example, she points out that almost everything he describes is brown – all the chocolate, the fudge, the walnuts, the squirrels (who in the manuscript pounce on Veruca like 'a flash of brown lightning', suggesting that Roald had native English reddish-brown squirrels in mind, rather than the American grey), which might give the illustrator a problem. And all the Easter eggs give the book a seasonal feel that might make it harder to sell.

They were all valuable, and potent, suggestions – although, she says now that 'he was going to get there anyway . . . If someone else hadn't alerted him, I'm quite sure he would have alerted himself. It was just lovely to be part of the game.' But perhaps her biggest contribution lies in how she encourages him – gives him permission, almost – to let his imagination soar and not be afraid of going too far. 'I'd like to see more humour, more light, Dahlesque touches throughout,' ends the letter. 'I hope some of my remarks will produce counter remarks in you that will stir you to flights of fancy to make the book take off and really fly as it undoubtedly will.'

And, of course, it did. By the end of the first week of publication in America in 1964, it had sold 10,000 copies and garnered almost uniformly rapturous reviews – including one from *The New York Times*, which said that the writer previously famed for his macabre short stories for adults had proved with *James and the Giant Peach* that he knew how to appeal to children and that with *Charlie and the Chocolate Factory* he had 'done it again, gloriously'. *Charlie* is described as 'fertile in invention, rich in humour [and] acutely observant . . . Mr Wonka is a Dickensian delight, and his factory, with its laughing, singing, tiny Oompa-Loompa workers, is sheer joy'. The paper later chose it as one of their books of the year. Among regional newspapers – as Donald Sturrock notes in his 2010 biography of Roald Dahl, *Storyteller* – only the *Boston Globe* disagreed, saying that some of the descriptions would give adult readers indigestion. The reviewer, however, did also have to admit that 'the young, with their stainless steel digestive systems, will take to it with relish'. The reviewer's counterpart at the *Boston Herald* compared the book to *Alice's Adventures in Wonderland* and said it 'should become a classic'.

Even the *Library Journal* – publication of record for librarians, who were at the time already (and would remain for many years) uneasy about Roald Dahl – said that 'his facility with the pen was unquestioned' although 'his taste and choice of language leave something to be desired'. That's a rave, though, compared with the journal's review of *James and the Giant Peach* when it first came out: 'The violent exaggeration of language and almost grotesque characterization impair the storytelling and destroy the illusion of reality and plausibility, which any good fantasy must achieve . . . Not recommended' (as reviewed by Ethel L. Heins, 15 November 1961).

Willy Wonka, illustrated by Quentin Blake.

Inside Charlie's Chocolate Factory

CHARLIE AND THE CHOCOLATE FACTORY. By Roald Dahl. Illustrated by Joseph Schindelman. 162 pp. New York: Alfred A. Knopf. $3.95.

_ For Ages 8 and Up._

CANDY for life and a personally conducted tour of Mr. Willy Wonka's top-secret chocolate factory, that was the sensational prize for buying a candy bar that contained a Golden Ticket. As millions of these delicious morsels are gobbled up every day and there are only five tickets, the odds against finding one were enormous, and public interest was feverish. Here is the exciting, hilarious and, incidentally, moral story of the prizewinners' adventures.

They were, alas, with one exception, singularly repulsive children. There was Augustus Gloop, whose sole activity was eating and who was so fat he could hardly see out of his eyes; and Veruca Salt, a spoiled brat who screamed for what she wanted until she got it; and Violet Beauregarde, who never stopped chewing gum, the little pest; and Mike Teevee, an obnoxious kid who watched Westerns, toted toy pistols and went "bang bang" all over the place. Ugh! They deserved — but never mind what they deserved, this is the story of what they got when they persisted in being objectionable, and anyway, their nastiness was outweighed by the niceness of Charlie Bucket, whose family was so poor he could only have one candy bar a year.

Roald Dahl, a writer of spine-chilling stories for adults, proved in "James and the Giant Peach" that he knew how to appeal to children. He has done it again, gloriously. Fertile in invention, rich in humor, acutely observant, he depicts fantastic characters who are recognizable as exaggerations of real types, and situations only slightly more absurd than those that happen daily, and he lets his imagination rip in fairyland.

The ta-ra in the press about the Golden Tickets, the fatuous remarks of the horrible children's parents, are wildly funny, while the break in starving Charlie's bad luck arouses a glow. Jovial, nimble Mr. Willy Wonka, tireless searcher for ever more scrumptious candies, is a Dickensian delight, and his factory, with its laughing, singing, tiny Oompa-Loompa workers, is sheer joy. It would not be fair to tell more. His secrets shall be sacred; you must read about them for yourself.

The illustrations show admirably the wistfulness of Charlie and the grotesqueness of the little horrors and their parents. My only regret is that these portraits are not in color. I fear that (except, of course, in libraries) crayons and paint boxes will be used for further adornment of an already lovely book. AILEEN PIPPETT.

However, public approbation, plus (one must assume) word of mouth among the juvenile population, translated into further sales. *Charlie* became a Book of the Month Club choice for children, and in September 1965 Roald's new editor at Knopf, Bob Bernstein, was writing to say that Roald could look forward to another 'very, very good Christmas'.

By 1968, *Charlie and the Chocolate Factory* had sold over 600,000 copies in the US and (together with the 250,000 copies sold of *James*) earned Roald Dahl a million dollars in royalties.

New York Times review of Charlie and the Chocolate Factory by Aileen Pippett, 25 October 1964.

In the UK, however, things were not going so smoothly. As had been the case with *James* a few years before, Roald's UK agents could not find a publisher there for *Charlie*. Despite its success across the pond, it was turned down by all the top-tier firms. He was keen to go to the other extreme and have both *Charlie* and *James* printed relatively cheaply in Czechoslovakia and sold – again, relatively cheaply – through any publisher who had sufficient distribution and marketing muscle. His UK agent Murray Pollinger was wholly against the idea, believing that this would leave Roald to be regarded as 'second-rate'. But Roald Dahl replied – perhaps more temperately in the flesh than he recorded later in a letter to Mike Watkins – 'Balls. NO mother who buys children's books has the faintest idea who publishes them.' In the days before branding had become so central to people's thinking this was probably truer than it is now – though it is probably still more true than any publisher would care to admit – but it was nevertheless a characteristically robust, stubborn and brave attitude to take.

Why did Chatto & Windus, Jonathan Cape, Collins, The Bodley Head and so many others in the UK say no to *Charlie*? Perhaps because its freewheeling, anarchic energy and delight in extremes sat less easily with the English literary establishment and sensibility, or 'priggish, obtuse stuffiness' as Roald Dahl called it in a letter to Alfred Knopf's wife Blanche in 1964. Publishing has always been a relatively staid and traditional business – and publishing for children even more so. Reservations about a perceived crudeness and tastelessness in Roald's work were in England not limited to librarians, and mere popularity among the young was not enough to countermand them. There was perhaps – whatever Roald Dahl preferred to call it – a greater sense of vocation that tempered the English editors' commercial imperative in the business of providing good books for children. 'As an editor, one has to like a book oneself,' said Judy Taylor (former publisher at The Bodley Head) to one of Roald's biographers, Jeremy Treglown. 'I could see that Dahl would be popular with children, but publishing for them has to involve more than that somehow.' Another editor told Donald Sturrock that she remained proud that she had turned the book down twice.

Taylor also recalls being put off by the tone of the letter from Roald's UK agents, which laid down conditions before anyone had expressed any interest in buying the book – an unusual tack for an author not yet very well known in Britain to take. So it is possible that Roald Dahl and those around him, knowing they had a US bestseller, had an air of arrogance about the venture that didn't help their cause.

After this flood of rejections, Roald got an unsolicited letter from Rayner Unwin, the co-founder of George Allen & Unwin publishers. His daughter Camilla had brought home American copies of *James* and *Charlie* that had been given to her by Tessa Dahl, her schoolfriend. Would Roald let his firm publish them in the UK?

Always an astute businessman, Roald Dahl sent a reply that led Unwin to understand that, although he was one among many interested parties, none of the others had yet made a 'proper commitment' to the books, and so the two men met. Roald told him about his idea to print and sell them cheaply and Unwin loved it. They entered into an unusual writer–publisher contract together, whereby instead of an advance and the normal royalty (when and if the advance was earned out) of 10% or 12.5%, Roald would get half of any profit made once Unwin's firm had recouped the printing costs.

It was a gamble that paid off. The books were published in 1967 and both sold out within weeks. So did the reprint, and the success encouraged Roald to start on another book for children – *Fantastic Mr Fox*, which would be published by Knopf in the US and by George Allen & Unwin in the UK.

Elaine Moss, reviewing *Charlie* in *The Times*, wrote: 'Humour has few classics but, unless I am very much mistaken, Roald Dahl's *Charlie and the Chocolate Factory* is destined for the roll of honour. It is the funniest children's book I have read in years; not just funny, but shot through with a zany pathos which touches the young heart.'

Well, quite.

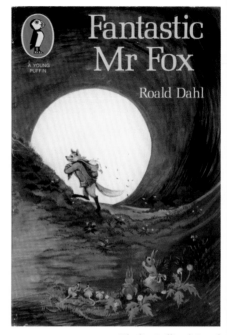

The first Puffin edition of *Fantastic Mr Fox*, illustrated by Jill Bennett (1974).

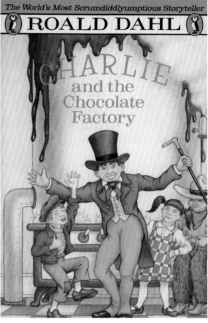

Various editions of *Charlie and the Chocolate Factory*, published by Puffin Books.

CLOCKWISE FROM TOP LEFT: 1973, illustrated by Faith Jaques (UK); 1988, cover illustration by Richard Egielski (US); 1997, illustrated by Quentin Blake (UK); 1998, illustrated by Quentin Blake (US).

Inside Charlie's Chocolate Factory

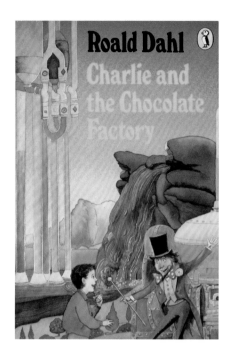

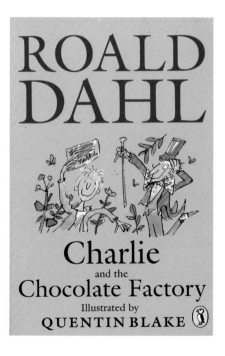

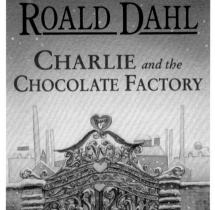

CLOCKWISE FROM TOP LEFT:
1985, illustrated by Michael
Foreman (UK); 2001,
illustrated by Quentin Blake
(UK); late 1980s, reprint of the
1985 edition with new cover
by Michael Foreman
(UK); 1998, illustrated by
Quentin Blake (UK).

Patricia Neal in evening dress with
Olivia, Tessa and Theo. This
photograph was taken by Roald Dahl
while they lived in New York (c.1961).

Inside Charlie's Chocolate Factory

The Late Sixties and Beyond

In 1965, Roald's wife, Patricia Neal, had a series of massive strokes while pregnant with their fifth child, Lucy. It was yet another terrible blow to strike the family in five years.

Patricia collapsed at home and was rushed to hospital. She had a lifesaving operation that night and remained in a coma for nearly three weeks. When she awoke, her right side was paralysed and she could barely speak. Her memory was gone. She looked and felt, Patricia said later in her autobiography, like 'an immense vegetable'.

Roald Dahl took the advice of Charles Carton, one of the top neurosurgeons in Los Angeles whom he had met to discuss bringing the Wade–Dahl–Till valve to the US, that Patricia should be verbally, mentally and physically stimulated and exercised as immediately, fully and unrelentingly as possible. To some, the programme of speech therapy, physiotherapy and every other kind of therapy that could be thought of looked almost abusive. Others understood what Roald was trying to do with his intensive programme of rehabilitative care for Patricia and had faith that it would work. Patricia herself suffered hugely but also benefited hugely. She gradually relearned how to walk and talk, and even, eventually, went back to work, despite a continuing struggle to remember lines. Reflecting after their divorce in 1983 on her years with him – volatile even before illness and bereavement intruded – she wrote, 'If I had not married Roald Dahl, I would have been denied my children, even my life, because he truly saved me and I will be forever grateful to him for that.'

By the end of the decade, Roald thought of himself no longer as the author of short stories for adults but primarily as a writer for children. His wife's health was improving, and there was interest in turning *Charlie and the Chocolate Factory* into a film, which brought a whole new round of attention to the book and to Roald.

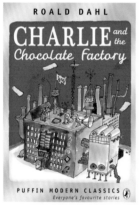

FROM TOP TO BOTTOM:
Puffin Modern Classic UK editions
(1997, 2010); Puffin Modern
Classic US edition (2003).

In 1969 news got out that the book was going to be made into a film starring Gene Wilder.

Meanwhile the civil-rights movement was reaching its zenith in the US. The campaign for equality for black people and other minority groups, begun in the 1950s, was now a powerful political and social force. It was dedicated to ending racism in all its forms around the world and especially in the US – a country that had officially abolished slavery barely a hundred years before, though the repercussions had continued long enough after that to remain within contemporary living memory. Martin Luther King Jr had been assassinated the year before but, far from weakening the movement as his killer hoped, the shocking loss had united and strengthened it.

Early in 1969, the film's producer, David Wolper, received a letter from the National Association for the Advancement of Colored People (NAACP), and director Mel Stuart was visited by a group of well-known black actors raising concerns about the 'racism' in *Charlie and the Chocolate Factory* – namely, the depiction of the Oompa-Loompas. They were described as 'a tribe of tiny, miniature pygmies . . . [from] . . . the very deepest and darkest part of Africa where no white man had ever been before'. Especially when coupled with the fact that Willy Wonka had brought them over to work in his factory (for payment in nothing but their – admittedly beloved – cacao beans), the whole thing created an image of slavery, which, although Roald had intended nothing of the kind, was nevertheless offensive to those who were trying to repair the harm caused by its legacy.

A revolution in thinking and cultural awareness had outpaced Roald Dahl, and indeed his agents and editors. As a young man, he had lived in Africa for several years as a Shell employee and then, after war broke out in 1939, as an RAF pilot, and he'd loved it there. The description of the Oompa-Loompas was the remnant of a section, eventually cut, in which Roald had pressed his knowledge of the land into service, giving Wonka a trip into the jungle to save the tribespeople from being thrown off their land by a vicious new plantation owner and starving to death.

Inside Charlie's Chocolate Factory

Wolper and Roald agreed immediately to change the Oompa-Loompas' appearance and they became the now-familiar, heavily stylized, green-haired, orange-skinned dwarves.

Rumours – wholly incorrect – started to spread that the NAACP would picket cinemas if the title wasn't changed, and that the words 'chocolate' (a derogatory term for black people) and 'Charlie' (hipster slang for 'white person' at the time) were the cause of the problem.

Eventually the title was changed to *Willy Wonka and the Chocolate Factory*. It was said to have been at the insistence of Quaker Oats, who were investing in the film as a way of marketing a new chocolate product and who wanted the emphasis to be as firmly on the inventor and his factory as possible. (But more on that later.) The description of the Oompa-Loompas in the book itself was rewritten in time for the second edition, and ever since they have remained tiny, long-haired, rosy-skinned, mashed-caterpillar haters and cacao lovers, rescued from almost certain death by snozzwangers in Loompaland.

Oompa-Loompas from *Willy Wonka and the Chocolate Factory* (1971).

'Nowhere in either of our reactions to *Charlie*,' says a letter from the assistant executive director of the NAACP, John A. Marsell, referring to his own feelings and those of June Shagaloff, the organization's education director, as the matter moved to a close, 'is there any reproach to Mr Dahl whose work we both admire. We are also aware that the book itself has proven enormously popular with children, and deservedly so.'

Unfortunately, it marked the beginning of a disquieting series of complaints for Roald about the book. The subset of librarians who had always seen him as a caterer to the lowest common denominator, giving children what they wanted rather than what they needed, seemed keen to use it as an excuse to keep him off their shelves at last. Four in Wisconsin for instance, as Sturrock notes, wrote to say they had discovered 'with great dismay' that the book contained 'passages with racist implications' that robbed 'the little black creatures . . . of all humanity'. Their own phraseology of course sounds impossibly patronizing to modern ears – further proof, perhaps, of how quickly sensibilities can change once a revolution in thought has started, and how easily good intentions can be later misinterpreted and misunderstood.

From the mid-seventies, the book and Roald really only grew in popularity. In the 1980s, during which he published most of his most famous books, including *The Twits*, *The BFG*, *The Witches* and *Matilda* and his two volumes of autobiography for children (*Boy* and *Going Solo*), one in three children's books bought in the UK was by Roald Dahl. Complaints died away – probably in part because detractors increasingly felt simply outnumbered but mainly, and more positively, because Roald's gifts as a storyteller, as a masterful, hugely original and inventive fabulist, came to be more widely and genuinely appreciated. Sometimes his critics got a purchase on him again – some saw misogyny in *George's Marvellous Medicine* and *The Witches*, for example, and he never lost his reputation as a maverick – but he was increasingly loved by adults, for his ability to enthral their offspring, and by children, for giving them books that felt, more than any others, like they were written by someone on their side. He wrote more and more books that captivated lovers of *Charlie* and then, as the years rolled on, their children – and now, of course, their children's children.

In 1972, Mike Watkins wrote to Roald to tell him that they had sold over 200,000 copies of his three books (*Charlie and the Chocolate Factory*, *James and the Giant Peach* and the new one, *Fantastic Mr Fox*) that year. 'Imagining that each copy must have a minimum of five readers,' he said, given that children share and that plenty of copies would have been bought by school and public libraries, 'you have given an enormous amount of pleasure.' How much more truly, wonderfully, gloriously, fantastically incomputable – forty-two years and nineteen books later – that calculation is today.

Inside Charlie's Chocolate Factory

Penguin Classics Deluxe edition, illustrated by cartoonist Ivan Brunetti (Penguin US, 2011).

Charlie and the Chocolate Factory was one of the titles selected for the Draw Your Own Cover series (Puffin, 2011), which inspired readers – both young and old – to create their own visions of Roald Dahl's classic story. Examples of readers' artwork can be seen on pages 196–197.

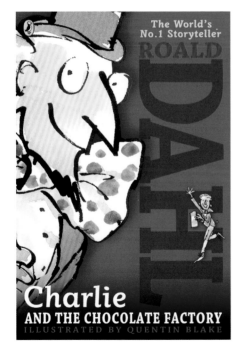

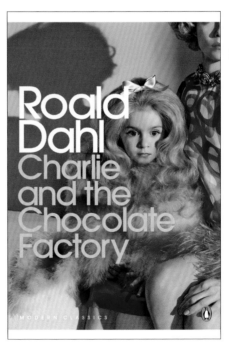

The latest UK edition (Puffin, 2013).

Penguin Modern Classics edition (Penguin, 2014).

TELEVISION CHOCOLATE
On Stage and Screen

PREVIOUS
SPREAD:
Artwork from a
promotional
poster for *Willy
Wonka and the
Chocolate Factory*
(1971).

RIGHT:
DVD cover of the
1971 film.

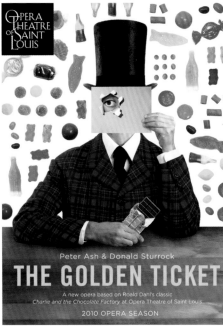

Introduction

Since publication, love for *Charlie and the Chocolate Factory* has only grown and its fame has spread further and further afield. *Charlie* has been published in more than fifty countries (and fifty-five languages) since first appearing in America fifty years ago.

But *Charlie* is no longer 'just' a book. It has been made into a film (twice), an opera, a play and a musical (directed by Sam Mendes and playing in London's West End as I write).

CLOCKWISE FROM TOP LEFT: Film poster, 2005.

Musical poster, London, 2013.

Poster for the operatic adaption by the Opera Theatre of Saint Louis, 2010.

Film poster, 1971.

Inside Charlie's Chocolate Factory

Willy Wonka and the Chocolate Factory

The most famous and influential of any of the adaptations of *Charlie and the Chocolate Factory* is of course the first of the two films made: 1971's *Willy Wonka and the Chocolate Factory*, directed by Mel Stuart and starring Gene Wilder.

As Stuart tells it in *Pure Imagination*, his account of the making of the film, his daughter Madeline – in an echo of Camilla Unwin and her father Rayner's discovery of the book a few years earlier – told him she had read it three times and wanted him to make it into a film. 'And have Uncle David sell it.' Uncle David was David Wolper, with whom Stuart had already made many major documentary films, such as *The Making of the President, 1960* (1963), *Four Days in November* (1964), *Wall Street: Where the Money Is* (1966) and *The Rise and Fall of the Third Reich* (1968). It probably takes a twelve-year-old's iron determination and limitless faith to present such a team with the story of a boy in a magical chocolate factory as their next project.

Before Wolper had even managed to read *Charlie*, he found himself in conversation with an advertising agent who had a client – Quaker Oats –

ABOVE LEFT:
Mel Stuart and the Oompa-Loompa actors.

ABOVE RIGHT:
Gene Wilder as Willy Wonka with the child actors.

I Am Curious
(oatmeal)

OLD FASHIONED QUAKER OATS

Recognizing the need for more "family oriented" motion pictures **THE QUAKER OATS COMPANY** *has formed an association with* **WOLPER PICTURES, LTD.** *to produce a series of feature films for the children's audience.*

DAVID L. WOLPER
President

MEL STUART
Vice President

A promotional poster from Quaker Oats, announcing their involvement with David Wolper.

who was looking for a project the food company could use to promote a new chocolate bar they were hoping to sell.

A deal was soon arranged. Quaker Oats would provide a $3m budget for the film, Paramount would distribute it, and Roald Dahl would write the script.

As Roald Dahl embarked on his first draft of the screenplay, Stuart, Wolper and Stan Margulies (another producer) began scouting locations and casting the main parts – and, as discussed in the previous chapter, they had to solve the difficulties thrown up by the original Oompa-Loompas. After filming started, Stuart wrote with relief to Wolper that the spur-of-the-moment solution he had come up with months ago was actually working: 'In spite of the make-up and the green hair, there is nothing grotesque about them.'

Filming, it was eventually decided, would take place in Munich. To help convey the skewed reality of the book, in which normal rules did not quite apply, Stuart wanted all the outside shots to take place somewhere not instantly familiar, somewhere that could seem to

Inside Charlie's Chocolate Factory

exist outside normal time and space. Munich was rarely used as a location (for British and American films at least) and seemed to have the universal storybook quality they were looking for. It also had a gasworks whose exterior, slightly modified by the art director Harper Goff, would make a very handy chocolate factory.

Gene Wilder and the Oompa-Loompa actors.

They found Augustus Gloop there too – otherwise known as twelve-year-old Michael Böllner, who was suitably rotund and in whose eventual mastery of English the dialogue coach had confidence. Stuart asked him to imagine what it was like to be stuck in a large tube. Böllner said he didn't know. 'I squeezed him like a roll of putty,' Stuart remembered later. '"You'll find out soon," I said.'

For Veruca Salt, they scoured the stage schools of England (where else would you look for a raging imperialist-to-be?) and Julie Dawn Cole got the part after three rounds of auditions. 'I had to read the book – which I hadn't read before – overnight between the first audition and the recall!' says Cole. 'And then I just wanted to see the Chocolate Room. *How* were they going to do it?' Stuart

Michael Böllner as Augustus Gloop, with Günter Meisner (Mr Slugworth) and Ursula Reit (Mrs Gloop).

ABOVE LEFT:
Julie Dawn Cole as
Veruca Salt.

ABOVE RIGHT:
Denise Nickerson as
Violet Beauregarde.

cast her 'because I could imagine her singing "I Want It Now!" and meaning every word'.

At the final audition, Cole – customarily a model of probity and a credit to her mother – lied about how much experience she had, 'completely unafraid of getting caught. I thought that if Mel found out . . . this very Veruca Salt-like behaviour would weigh in my favour rather than against.'

Cole met Roald Dahl when she had to fly out early to do a recording of her song 'I Want It Now'. 'He was very nice and charming to me but – I think "brusque" would be the word for him. He didn't particularly make allowances for children –

he expected you to come up to his level in conversation,' she remembers. 'Oh – and he was very, *very* tall!'

Denise Nickerson, who at thirteen had already been acting for over a decade in theatre and on television, got the role of Violet Beauregarde – partly for her acting ability and partly for her round, baby cheeks. Stuart thought she looked just right for someone destined for life as a blueberry!

'It was my first opportunity to work with kids my age – a true delight, having always only worked with adults before. The set, our hotel – I was living in a real fairy tale!'

Her memory of the author is similar to Cole's, that he was a

Inside Charlie's Chocolate Factory

fabulous figure from a distance, and he also complimented her on her portrayal as 'his Violet', Nickerson remembers, once she had screwed up the courage to approach him.

Ebullient eleven-year-old Paris Themmen had acted in commercials and on stage and, although he was young, Stuart thought he had the perfect brattiness for the Mike Teavee part. (The later consensus on set was that this was true. 'Four of them are wonderful,' said Wilder in a television interview during filming, 'and one of them I'm going to throw through a window tomorrow.' But he was eleven. And a great Mike Teavee. And Wilder's was an appropriately

Dahlesque rendering of the situation into one funny – heartfelt, but funny – line.)

Charlie was the most difficult part to cast. Where do you find a child capable of projecting the necessary goodness, of being the still, quiet centre of the Wonka storm and yet not coming across (as Roald put it in a letter to Peggy Caulfield, his agent's assistant) as a 'boring little bugger'? They found him at the children's branch of the Cleveland Playhouse, Ohio, in the shape of twelve-year-old Peter Ostrum. He was told he had the part ten days before shooting began and he had to set off immediately for five months in Munich.

ABOVE LEFT:
Paris Themmen as
Mike Teavee.

ABOVE RIGHT:
Peter Ostrum as
Charlie Bucket.

Joel Grey.

Fred Astaire.

What About Wonka?

The all-singing, all-dancing, all-Tony-Award-winning stage actor Joel Grey was the man they first and most seriously considered for the part of Willy Wonka. He could do it all, but eventually Stuart decided that he just wasn't physically imposing enough for a man he envisaged as a father figure to the children. If any of the child actors had a growth spurt during filming, they could easily end up taller than the five-foot-five star.

They spent another week looking at alternatives. They heard later that Fred Astaire had wanted the part, but he had not approached either Stuart or Wolper. Perhaps the then seventy-two-year-old knew in his heart what Stuart would have said – that he was too old. Difficult too, perhaps, to envisage Astaire, the epitome of gentlemanly charm, mustering the necessary eccentricity and acidity for their version of Willy Wonka.

At the end of that week of auditions, Wilder walked in. His main screen appearances so far had been in a supporting role in *Bonnie and Clyde* (1967), co-starring in *The Producers* (1968), which hadn't yet become the big

Inside Charlie's Chocolate Factory

hit it would be later on, and starring in *Start the Revolution Without Me* (1970). As Wolper and Stuart both tell it, they knew at once that they could stop looking. 'His inflection was perfect. He had the sardonic, demonic edge that we were looking for,' said Stuart. 'Perfect,' said Wolper in *Producer*, his autobiography, 'does not begin to describe it. The role fit him tighter than Jacques Cousteau's wetsuit.'

Wolper in vain tried to stop Stuart from betraying his enthusiasm to the actor so that the producer could negotiate a deal on his salary, but Stuart ran out into the hall anyway to tell him that he *was* Wonka and that he had the part. This is why producers hate creatives.

Wilder signed up on one condition – that his entrance would comprise him hobbling out of the factory and limping painfully slowly towards the ticket winners. At the last moment, he would slip, fall, execute a perfect somersault and end up standing triumphantly in front of them. 'Because from that time on,' he explained in his autobiography, *Kiss Me Like a Stranger*, 'no one will know if I'm lying or telling the truth.'

Gene Wilder.

Dear Mel   July 23rd

I've just received the costume sketches.
I'll tell you everything I think, without
censoring, and you take from my
opinion what you like.

I assume that the designer took
his impressions from the book and
didn't know, naturally, who would be
playing Willy. And I think, for a
character in general, they're lovely
sketches.

I love the main thing — the velvet
jacket — and I mean to show by my
sketch the exact same color.
But I've added two large pockets
to take away from the svelt, feminine
line. (Also in case of a few props.)

I also think the vest is both
appropriate and lovely.

And I love the same white, flowing
shirt and the white gloves. Also the lighter
colored inner silk lining of the jacket.

OPPOSITE:
First page of a letter from Gene Wilder to Mel Stuart, discussing the sketches for Willy Wonka's outfit, in particular the colour and the inclusion of pockets – 'in case of a few props' (1970).

LEFT:
Gene Wilder in his Willy Wonka outfit.

Imagination Come to Life

So – as Harper Goff was busy drawing up plans and having the chocolate river and waterfall built in the Bavaria Film studios in Munich – the stage was, almost literally, set. The only problem was the script.

Screenwriting is a very different art from other kinds of writing. Some brilliant authors of novels find they can turn their pens to it as readily as they do ordinary prose narrative – Raymond Chandler did, Larry McMurtry did, and the Nobel and (twice) Pulitzer Prize-winning William Faulkner really did, managing to write *The Sound and the Fury* (1929), *As I Lay Dying* (1930) and *Absalom, Absalom!* (1936) before knocking out the likes of *To Have and Have Not* (1944) and *The Big Sleep* (1946) for Hollywood. Roald Dahl also had success in this field, penning the screenplays of *You Only Live Twice* (1967) and *Chitty Chitty Bang Bang* (1968). Other equally brilliant writers, like F. Scott Fitzgerald, Aldous Huxley and Vladimir Nabokov, find they cannot.

There are additional problems if a writer is trying to adapt his own work. Nine times out of ten, he or she is simply too close to the material to see what needs to be done to make it accessible on screen. Which makes sense. After all, if he or she had ever envisaged the story as a film instead of a book, it would have been written in that form in the first place. To the creator, it is what it is. And it is an axiom of movie-making that you can't film the book. You need to be able to rip it apart, identify the truly vital elements of the story, rearrange them, beef up some and

Inside Charlie's Chocolate Factory

tone down others, to account for the differences between a movie-going and a reading audience and the different emphases the screen gives to things compared to the printed page. And then you have to find a way to show it, by translating description into visual scenes or dialogue that the characters can say realistically, plausibly, as seemingly entirely natural extensions of themselves.

On top of all that, *Charlie and the Chocolate Factory* presents a structural challenge to a dramatist. Most tales in books, and especially on stage or screen, have three acts: a set-up, a series of complications and then resolution. A reader might feel that *Charlie* has two: the introduction to all the characters as they find the Golden Tickets; and the tour of the factory in which all those characters (bar Charlie, of course) are dispatched in ways that befit their particular flaws and Charlie is rewarded for his virtue.

This hardly matters in the book. Roald Dahl's authoritative voice admits no possible objections. You are completely caught up – especially as a young reader, though I have empirically proven that it still happens when you are thirty-eight and reading it for the 876th time too – in the incredible, voluptuous, wildly imaginative scenes whizzing past your eyes and sparking off others in your head, entranced by the mad energy of it all and enchanted by its difference from the sober, industrious, 'good' books put before you by teachers, parents and librarians.

But . . . up on screen, you need something else. Most of what was written

ABOVE:
Images from the
1971 film.

David Seltzer, who wrote part of the screenplay for *Charlie*, is shown here directing on the set of a later film.

for two weeks, where he was locked in a hotel room to write every day and only allowed out for meals. At the end of the fortnight, Seltzer flew home exhausted. Roald Dahl remains the only writer credited on the film, but Seltzer said later – after he had become a successful screenwriter in Hollywood, with the likes of *The Omen* (1976), *Punchline* (1988) and *Bird on a Wire* (1990) under his belt – that his two weeks there was the best training a young screenwriter could have had.

When Roald heard that Seltzer was – in movie parlance – 'writing behind him', he was furious. Stuart had to fly over to London and let him see the new script. Roald read it and gave his approval but remained deeply upset and demoralized by the whole experience, which may explain at least in part his lasting animosity towards the finished product.

in a book is made visible: one picture of a chocolate waterfall may represent a thousand words of description but is taken in at a glance and more content is needed to fill the gap.

Roald revised his script, working in suggestions from Stuart and Wolper each time, but never resolved all its problems to their satisfaction.

While Roald was working on the second draft, they hired writer Bob Kaufman to add some comic interludes around the discovery of the five Golden Tickets.

During the third rewrite, they brought in a twenty-five-year-old writer called David Seltzer to do some additional work on it. They ended up flying him to Munich

Inside Charlie's Chocolate Factory

The children and parents
enter the Chocolate Room for
the first time, led by Willy
Wonka, in the 1971 film.

The Lights, the Cameras, the Action

Writerly misery aside, it was a happy set. For Stuart, although the
Quaker Oats people were less flexible than a studio in granting more
money to overcome logistical or actor problems, they were also very
much less interfering than the average Hollywood executive – always
the way to a director's heart. The children were giddy at the strangeness
and exoticness of it all, to say nothing of the daily confectionery spoils
they managed to liberate from the set and various crew members.

   To help them with their performances, Stuart shot as much as he
could chronologically. He also went to great lengths to capture genuine
reactions from his young actors. They didn't know, for example, that
the gold-painted hands that acted as hooks for them to hang their coats
on when they first arrived in the factory were real until the gilded
ornaments reached out and grabbed for them. Nor that Gene Wilder
was going to rise to such a demented pitch as he recited his poem on the
boat ride, to end on an unearthly scream. 'I really thought he had gone
mad,' remembered Denise Nickerson years later. And the actor playing

Peter Ostrum
as Charlie.

Julie Dawn Cole
as Veruca Salt.

Slugworth, whose attempts to bribe the children to betray Wonka's industrial secrets had been introduced to give the film a sense of mystery the book didn't have, stayed away from them as much as possible so that they were indeed a little bit afraid of him (and the scar on his face, which they didn't know was fake).

But, most vitally of all, the set of the Chocolate Room, with its river, its waterfall, its sweets, its colours, its sugared flowers, dyed marzipan fruits and mushrooms pumped full of whipped cream, and its chocolate-filled pumpkins and chocolate-hung trees, was kept from them (at least as far as Stuart knew; in fact, Julie Dawn Cole, who'd arrived early to rehearse her big number, had been given a peek at an early version by a stagehand before Stuart had forbidden it). They were encouraged to run off and explore without specific direction – to be guided by what was edible or not.

'I tried quite a lot of it!' says Cole, recalling the sweets. 'And it was just the most magical thing to see. It's still a wonderful memory.'

Inside Charlie's Chocolate Factory

'The view from the top of the stairs was not nearly as unbelievable on film as it was in reality,' Denise Nickerson says today.

It's a testament to the brilliance of Roald Dahl's original idea (and description) and Stuart's depiction of it on screen that, however old you are, I suspect you spent at least a fleeting moment longing to be there in the Chocolate Room with them, running through that paradisiacal place. I hope you did anyway. I virtually wept with envy writing about it.

If you do ever end up there, by the way, of the chocolate bars available Cole recommends the Scrumdiddlyumptious ones – 'they were chocolate-covered Turkish Delight' – over both the Whipple-scrumptious Fudgemallow Delights ('like Wagon Wheels') and plain Wonka Bars, which were solid Hershey's chocolate. You're welcome.

The only major departure from the descriptions in the book of the rooms where the children meet their various fates was that the Nut Room had to become the Golden Egg Room, populated by animated geese

Oompa-Loompas in the Golden Egg room, where Veruca meets her end in the 1971 film.

instead of squirrels. Finding a way of either training or faking forty bushy-tailed rodents was something Stuart couldn't manage with the technology and limited time available.

The chronological filming meant that very soon Michael Böllner was facing the cold, brown mixture of water (150,000 gallons), chocolate ice-cream powder, salt conditioner (to control the smell) and a dash of the chemical that controls the foaming of shampoo (to

Augustus Gloop falls into
the chocolate river and is
sucked up the chute.

counteract the whitening froth the waterfall produced) that constituted
the chocolate river, and required to dive in. He remembers:

> *We tried it a whole day and my clothes were wet. I had
> three sets of clothing but the dry ones were reserved for the
> real shots. And it was very dangerous as the river was just
> fifteen centimetres deep. There was only a hole of a square
> metre [invisible under the water], which I had to aim at.
> Every time I was afraid I'd hurt my head.*

The river scene was of course followed by the scene in which Augustus
does indeed learn what it's like to get sucked up a giant tube. 'They put
the tube around me by crane and I could not move. Then they pumped
water in it up to my face. My life depended on the guys who operated
the water tap.'

If it helps, he sounds quite sanguine when he talks about it now.

So, apart from writerly misery AND Augustus Gloop's patient
suffering, it was a happy set. We should probably also mention Denise

Nickerson (Violet) too – for the final part of her en-blueberrying, she was sandwiched between two halves of a giant Styrofoam ball (a centrepiece in the shape of her body had been cut out beforehand) so that only her head, hands and feet were poking out. But, because she was wider than the Oompa-Loompas were tall, they couldn't see where they were going when they had to roll her out of the Inventing Room and kept banging her head into the door jamb. And when everybody broke for lunch she had to stay there because it would have taken too long to get her out and back into costume. She recalls:

Violet Beauregarde is turned into a giant blueberry.

> *Mel Stuart assigned a man, who only spoke German, to roll me 180 degrees every five minutes. When my head hung down looking at the floor, I was able to sip a milkshake through a straw with my 'German roller' holding the cup to my mouth. And that is how Violet spent her lunch break that day!*

One by one, the children finished their scenes (though only after thirty-six takes before the sequence in 'I Want it Now', in which Veruca Salt has to wrap cellophane round Willy Wonka and a tower of boxes falls, came out perfectly – a number which Julie Dawn Cole says remained her record throughout her acting career) and went home. When it was just Gene Wilder and Peter Ostrum left, they would often have lunch together and walk back to the set sharing a bar of chocolate.

When it came to the final scenes, Stuart saw the set for Wonka's office – which was then perfectly normal – and decided that this didn't suit the

Wonka's 'half' office.

In the Great Glass Elevator.

OPPOSITE:
Poster for the French release of the 1971 film.
Illustrated by Barbara Baranowska.

eccentric confectioner at all. So he ordered that everything be cut in half. And it was – including a coffee machine that a member of the crew took a saw to before he realized that it wasn't part of the set but actually full of . . . well, coffee for the crew. The light bulb remained whole, incidentally, because they couldn't work out a way, at least at such short notice, to cut through it and still have it light up. So the 'meaning' of the half-office – long pored over by fans in forums across the internet – is, according to Stuart, 'that none of it makes sense. But it makes great nonsense.'

In the shooting script, the film ends with Willy Wonka, Charlie and Grandpa Joe setting off in the Great Glass Elevator for Charlie's house. The very final line is Grandpa Joe crying 'Yippee!' They were all set up to film it on one of the last days of the shoot when Stuart realized that this was no exit line for his film. 'Find David Seltzer!' he cried. 'We need an ending!' Well, Seltzer, it transpired after many phone calls between Munich and David Wolper's office in LA, had not just gone home to the States to recuperate after his hotel incarceration; he had gone to Maine. An isolated part of Maine, and to a particularly isolated cabin therein. It was near a communal phone nailed to a tree. If anyone was passing when it rang, he or she would pick it up and – hopefully – try to track down the person the caller needed.

Stuart rang the number. Seltzer happened to be walking by. Stuart told him the problem. Seltzer asked how long he had to solve it. 'About three minutes,' replied Stuart. 'OK,' the writer replied. He laid the phone down and paced around for a minute then came back on the line. 'Here it is,' he said. 'Have Wonka say ominously to Charlie: "Charlie, don't forget what happened to the man who suddenly got everything he ever wanted." Have Charlie nervously reply, "What happened?" Then have Wonka say, "He lived happily ever after."'

Inside Charlie's Chocolate Factory

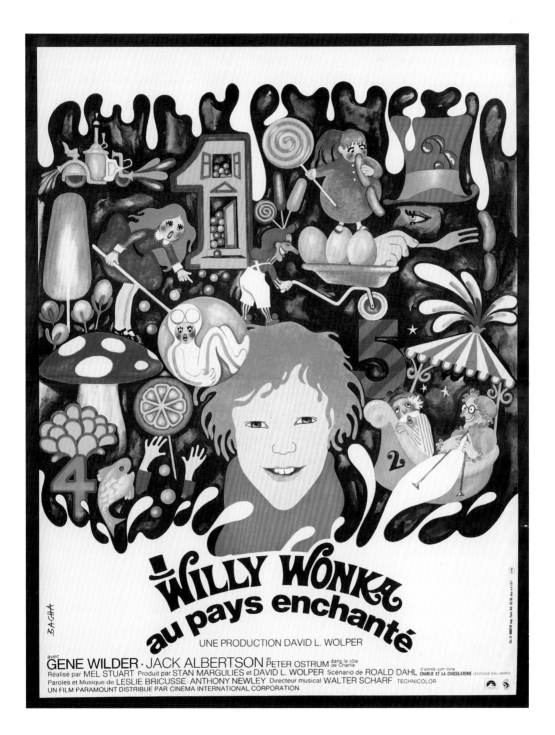

Love or hate the film or the ending (and Roald disliked both, the latter in particular), you gotta love that story.

But would the audience love the film?

Willy Wonka and the Chocolate Factory premiered in July 1971, in London and New York – where Gene Wilder dressed up as Willy Wonka and handed out ice creams and bars of chocolate from the Wonkamobile.

The reviews came in, and were less than scrumdiddlyumptious. In many ways they echoed the criticisms Roald Dahl had faced when he first published the book. 'Cynical and sadistic,' *Daily Variety* called it. The mighty Pauline Kael in the equally mighty *New Yorker* called it 'stilted and frenetic, like Prussians at play'. Another reviewer huffed that 'Mr Stuart obviously dislikes chocolate.' (For the record, he didn't, but Julie Dawn Cole did. That scene where Veruca breaks through the pumpkin and starts enthusiastically scooping its chocolate insides into her mouth? That's acting, folks.)

As with the book in 1964, some reviewers 'got' it – Roger Ebert (*Chicago Sun Times* critic) foremost among them. 'This weekend I saw the best family film I've seen in four years on this job, and probably the best film of its sort since *The Wizard of Oz* . . . It is everything that family movies usually claim to be but aren't: delightful, funny, scary, exciting and most of all, a genuine work of imagination.'

Alas, such glowing terms were not enough to persuade many people to go and see the film. It was trounced in its opening weekend by *Ben*, a sequel to *Willard*, a story about a plague of telepathic rats.

And Quaker Oats never did manage to create a decent chocolate bar.

Inside Charlie's Chocolate Factory

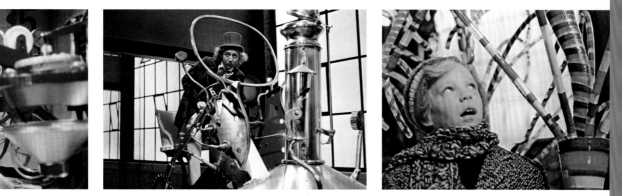

They had problems with the formula for the planned Willy Wonka's Peanut Butter Oompa-Loompa Cups and gave it up as a bad job before it even reached the shops. (Sometimes life in the Inventing Room gives you Everlasting Gobstoppers. Sometimes it gives you insoluble peanut-butter-based problems.) Paramount quickly lost interest in their property and chose not to divert any more resources towards marketing and publicizing the film, and it appeared to die a quiet death.

Except, of course, it didn't.

A few years later, it began playing on network television in the US – maybe once or twice a year, around Christmas and Thanksgiving. It picked up quite a few fans via a medium that didn't require anyone to travel to a cinema, or take a chance with a ticket to a panned film, but reached into the homes of 270 million people instead.

In the 1980s, cable television arrived and *Willy Wonka and the Chocolate Factory* found another outlet, and another audience took it to their hearts.

Then came video and the same thing happened. Add to that a burgeoning nostalgic glow around the film as kids who grew up with it came of age, had their own children and gradually took over the echelons of the entertainment industry, and Willy Wonka's shining place in the film firmament was assured. The internet too, as we shall see in a later chapter, has given it additional publicity and life.

This was all, obviously, a great vindication for Stuart and even more of a delight to David Wolper, who in 1977 had become a corporate director at Warner Bros and persuaded Quaker Oats to sell their 50% share in the film to him, meaning every dime of profit since has gone to the studio. And this is why creatives – and possibly cereal makers – hate producers.

ABOVE: Images from the 1971 film.

The Cast of *Willy Wonka and the Chocolate Factory*

Rusty Goffe, the original cartwheeling Oompa-Loompa. After *Willy Wonka and the Chocolate Factory*, he appeared in *Flash Gordon* and *Willow*, as well as playing various goblins in five of the Harry Potter films.

FROM LEFT TO RIGHT: Charlie was Peter Ostrum's only film role and he is now a vet in New York state; Michael Böllner (Augustus Gloop) also gave up acting and now runs his own tax accounting firm in Munich.

Inside Charlie's Chocolate Factory

FROM LEFT TO RIGHT:
Denise Nickerson (Violet Beauregarde) retired from acting in 1978, at the age of twenty-one, and is currently an accountant in Colorado.

Paris Themmen (Mike Teavee) proved to have flair as a business entrepreneur, founding a travel service for backpackers after he graduated from university, and has even worked for Walt Disney Imagineering (which builds and designs the theme parks). These days he is a commercial casting agent in Los Angeles.

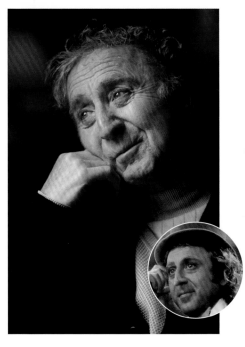

FROM LEFT TO RIGHT:
Julie Dawn Cole (Veruca Salt) continues to have a successful career in theatre and television, and she is also a qualified fitness instructor and psychotherapist.

Gene Wilder (Willy Wonka) has enjoyed a stellar acting career, receiving critical acclaim and is one of Hollywood's leading comic actors.

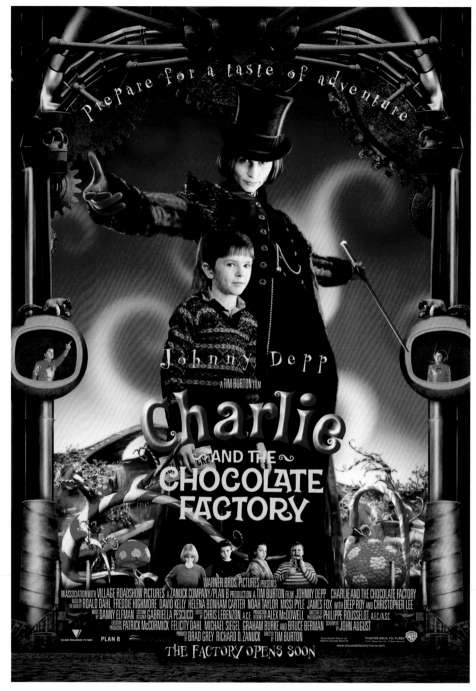

Poster for the 2005 film.

Inside Charlie's Chocolate Factory

The Second Film

Roald Dahl's experience of film adaptation the first time round was unhappy, though at least he did not cry during the premiere, as a horrified P. L. Travers did when she saw Disney's version of her bestseller *Mary Poppins* – released in 1964, the same year that *Charlie* was published – which she hated until the day she died. Roald didn't agree to another film for almost ten years until he gave permission for *Danny the Champion of the World*, *The Witches* and the animated version of *The BFG*. *Danny* and *The BFG* films came out in 1989, a year before Roald died.

In the mid-1990s, Roald's widow Liccy (whom he had married in 1983) met Tim Burton, who wanted to co-produce a stop-motion animation version of *James and the Giant Peach*. When she asked him why, Burton replied, 'Because it was the only thing that gave me hope as a child.' 'And I,' Liccy says, 'was seduced!' The film was liked by both the public and the family, which stood Burton in good stead when the question of making another film of *Charlie and the Chocolate Factory* arose.

At the very end of the 1990s and beginning of 2000, Gary Ross (writer of *Big*, and writer and director of *Pleasantville*, *Seabiscuit* and later *The Hunger Games*) signed up with Warner Bros to direct a new *Charlie*. And Scott Frank (writer of television series *The Wonder Years* as well as *Malice*, *Get Shorty*, *Out of Sight* and *Minority Report*) was hired to write a script. He completed two drafts; they were 'handsome enough, but they didn't jump in the way I would have liked them to', he explained to an IGN

Danny the Champion of the World (1989).

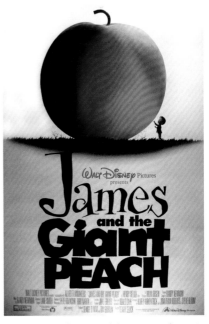

Film poster of *James and the Giant Peach* (1996).

interviewer in 2001. Unfortunately Frank didn't feel that he was anywhere nearer solving the structural problems of the book or that he could find a way to make Willy Wonka 'relevant . . . in this day and age of Harry Potter, Lemony Snicket (for my mind, the new Roald Dahl) and kids with guns'. His heart no longer in it, Frank stepped down from the project.

Gary Ross also left the project and various other director–writer permutations followed but nothing quite worked out until, to Liccy Dahl's delight, Tim Burton signed up to direct. He hired John August to write another script for what was now a $150-million-dollar film. 'I sat down with Tim in a restaurant in Santa Monica,' says August, 'and he said, "I want everything in the book and just as much more as [the film] needs to make sense."'

August had read *Charlie and the Chocolate Factory* when he was eight and he'd loved it so much that when his third-grade teacher asked her class to write letters to famous people he chose Roald Dahl. 'Everyone else chose Jimmy Carter!' And, as he did with all the children who wrote to him, Roald Dahl had replied. He sent one of his personalized postcards rather than a full bespoke response (impossible to produce for all the thousands of children who wrote to him every year), but August has kept the card to this day as a reminder of the time

**Gipsy House
Great Missenden
Buckinghamshire
England**
14th May, 1979.

Dear John

Thank you so much for your letter. I liked getting it. I'm afraid this is a very short reply. I wish I could send you a long one -- but there are such a lot of letters to be answered, and there is a new book to be written, and a million other things to be done, so please forgive me.

With love from

Roald Dahl

Roald Dahl's postcard to John August (1979).

Inside Charlie's Chocolate Factory

the nascent writer realized that actual, real people wrote books. (History does not record, incidentally, how many people received a reply from President Carter.)

There was no question as to who Burton would ask to play Wonka. It was a part tailor-made for his long-time muse and collaborator Johnny Depp. 'I think I probably let him finish about a sentence and a half before I blurted out the words "I'm in!"' said Depp in his foreword for *Burton on Burton*.

The film was cast. Burton wanted to use the four-feet-four-inch-tall actor Deep Roy with whom he had worked on previous films *Big Fish* (2003) and *The Corpse Bride* (2005), so, with the help of CGI, Roy agreed to take on the roles of the entire 165-strong Oompa-Loompa tribe.

The biggest problem, however, proved to be finding a Charlie, until Depp suggested a young actor he had worked with on *Neverland* (2004) – Freddie Highmore. Like Peter Ostrum, he projects an innate goodness without seeming weak, smug or boring and gives an equally (quietly) enchanting performance. Burton spoke admiringly of his 'gravity' as

Johnny Depp as Willy Wonka, on set with Tim Burton.

Deep Roy as the Oompa-Loompas, multiplied with the help of CGI.

Freddie Highmore as Charlie.

'something you can't tell an actor to do, they either have that or they don't. And Freddie just has an intelligence and simplicity in his acting; he really doesn't have false moments because he's not a false person.'

Six months of shooting ended in December 2004 and audiences got to see the finished product (and buy associated chocolate bars launched by Nestlé in the UK at the same time and with more success than poor Quaker Oats) when it opened in July 2005.

The film is true to Burton's wish to have everything that was in the book. In that sense, it was far more faithful to Roald's creation than the 1971 film was – though whether everything that was added to the 2005 version was necessary to make sense of the story is a question we'll come back to.

In addition to all the key scenes of the Chocolate Room and so on inside the factory, and the fates of the four children, Mr Bucket works in

Inside Charlie's Chocolate Factory

a toothpaste factory. (There was no Mr Bucket at all for Peter Ostrum's *Charlie*, so that Willy Wonka could function as a father figure as well as mentor to the boy – though in both films the children only get to bring along one companion each. 'There are just too many people in that factory!' says John August.) And we see Wonka journeying through Loompaland and finding his new workforce. We even see the Oompa-Loompa who is testing the hair-restoring toffee. Poor thing.

There is no Slugworth subplot, Wonkamobile or fizzy lifting drinks such as Stuart added to his version. And of course technology had advanced by then to allow the Nut Room to remain exactly that, instead of needing to be transformed into a roomful of golden-egg-laying geese. Forty heavily educated, real squirrels were in fact used in the filming (which, really, makes you wonder if Stuart mislaid his

ambition in Munich), but some parts still had to be added by computer and animatronic puppets later on.

However, there was still at least one problem technology couldn't solve. 'Obviously,' Freddie Highmore recalls, 'the chocolate river wasn't real chocolate, and began to smell pretty awful after a few weeks under the studio's lights!' The Chocolate Room's spell, nevertheless, endured:

> *As a child, I felt being on a film set was quite magical . . . The sets were all real and easily as spectacular as I'd imagined [when reading the book] . . . Of course, filming involves lots of repeating of action but if you're having fun it is just a chance to have more. The boat in* Charlie, *for example, was held on giant hydraulics for the close-ups and would buck us in all directions at great speed. It was like an amazing fairground ride and we kids never wanted to get off . . . It was a very happy shoot.*

Inside Charlie's Chocolate Factory

whipping a cow
for whipped cream.

Pages from Tim Burton's
sketchbooks for *Charlie and
the Chocolate Factory.*

Television Chocolate

Tim Burton's *Charlie and the Chocolate Factory* took $56,178,450 in its opening weekend – the fifth highest gross for 2005 – and received largely positive reviews. *Empire* magazine called it 'Witty, wonderful and wildly imaginative, Burton's first proper "family movie" since *Pee-Wee's Big Adventure* delivers a sugar rush that'll last for days.' *The New York Times* said it succeeded in doing 'what far too few films aimed primarily at children even know how to attempt any more, which is to feed – even to glut – the youthful appetite for aesthetic surprise.' And Roger Ebert thought 'the visual invention is a wonderment . . . The kids, their adventures and the song and dance numbers are so entertaining' – although he also spoke for many others when he added that Depp's version of Willy Wonka was 'strange . . . not fatal to the movie, although it's at right angles to it'.

It stayed at number one at the box office for two weeks and its total gross of just over $475m was the eighth highest worldwide that year (seventh highest in the US) and the fifty-eighth highest ever (at that time). It was nominated for an Oscar, a Golden Globe, several BAFTAs and a Grammy. Not a bad return on either the financial or creative investments made.

And yet. And yet. In the years that have elapsed since then, it shows no signs of having been taken to heart in the way the book has been or that the earlier film was. Why?

When David Seltzer was asked why he thought the 1971 version had gained such a following over the years (aside from the external factors like the growth of video and so on – which cannot, after all, be the whole story otherwise *Ben* and *Willard* would loom as large as the chocolate factory in our collective consciousness) he said:

> *We were really a bunch of amateurs flying by the seat of our pants and I think the film reflects that . . . It has that kind of energy. It's not the function of sitting down and intellectualizing . . . It's the function of cardboard . . . Scotch Tape . . . [the spirit of] 'let's put on a show'. It's not the result of a ton of money . . . I think that's the flavour of what makes the movie so vital.*

OPPOSITE: Posters for the 2005 film, featuring the main characters.

Inside Charlie's Chocolate Factory

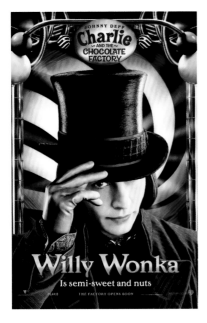

In other words, the 1971 film is still recognizably a labour of love, which gives it something you can't aim for or produce to order – it gives it charm. And it means the film captures the essence of the book in a way that goes deeper than a simple replication of its set pieces; it has the same sense of confidence and brio as the original book. Just as Roald wrote and invented and punished and rewarded his characters as he saw fit, so Stuart *et al.* made imaginative leaps, took bold decisions and did things that didn't quite make sense but still made great nonsense.

Things had changed in the film – and outside – world by the time the second film was made. Everything from coffee-making and cupcake-baking to the mainstream entertainment world had become slicker and more professional. Amateurism is rarely acceptable now unless it can be packaged as a charming oddity – like in *The Great British Bake Off* and its ilk – or co-opted by conglomerates to lend a spurious sense of vitality and edginess to their brands and products (*The X Factor* takes the lead here).

Burton's *Charlie and the Chocolate Factory* is indubitably one impossibly talented director's vision, and one in which he was keen to add as much realism as possible (from the plants in the Chocolate Room, some of which were real, if often then painted, to those forty squirrels in the Nut Room), but it is also (and this is in no way a criticism, just the noting of an inevitability) a product of its time. It looks finished. It looks done. It looks like careful, note-perfect work. And with that comes a degree of what psychologists call the shallowness of affect. You just can't feel too strongly about it. Your imagination has nothing to grab on to, no gaps to plug, no room to manoeuvre. It is frictionless entertainment. In this, of course, the experience is as unlike reading Roald Dahl as it can possibly be.

In 1971, Roald's anarchic spirit was embodied in the cast and crew's willingness to throw themselves wholeheartedly into the enterprise, to make do and make the best of what they had. By contrast, Burton's highly controlled and polished film seems to enlist the essence of nonconformity as a justification for making changes. In *Burton on Burton*, he notes: 'We added new elements . . . but I always felt comfortable that everything was in the spirit of his work . . . it's an interpretation, and there's an anarchic spirit there, so you kind of take it a few different ways.'

Inside Charlie's Chocolate Factory

The greatest change, perhaps, that Burton made to his source material is to envisage Willy Wonka not as an eccentric adult but as one of the children – a genius in one area of life only and in the rest a marked case of arrested development.

Where Stuart introduced dramatic tension via Slugworth – picking up on the brief mention of him near the beginning of the book when Grandpa Joe explains that Wonka shut up shop because of industrial spies – Burton chose to do so by giving Wonka a mysterious past. This turned out to be an estrangement from his father, a dentist (played, wonderfully, by Christopher Lee), who wouldn't let his son eat sweets, let alone pursue his dreams of becoming the world's greatest chocolatier. At the end of the film, Wonka meets his father again, sees that his father has been following his career through all the years they have been separated, and they are instantly reconciled.

All of this weights the film quite differently from the first version and from the book. One of the glories of *Willy Wonka and the Chocolate Factory* in general and of Gene Wilder's Willy Wonka in particular is that it all simply . . . exists. It manages, like the book, to create a factory

Johnny Depp as Willy Wonka, outside his factory.

Gene Wilder as Willy Wonka.

world that floats free of quotidian trappings and concerns. Willy Wonka just *is*. Gene Wilder's interpretation of him is *sui generis* – a true one-off, a fascinating oddity you would be hard put to say was influenced by anyone or anything. Even if the lines aren't always the same as Roald's, Wonka's mercurial nature is the one that he created. Wilder's Wonka, like Roald's, can turn on a dime and head off in a different direction and you must just do your grinning, panting best to keep up. You revel in him as he revels in his perfect life in the factory – just as the reader and character do in the book. He is a man who has already won. When Charlie inherits the factory, our young hero inherits – we feel – that perfect freedom too, the perfect world in which to be himself. And who among us, watching or reading, doesn't want a gorgeous, creamy chunk of that?

Burton/Depp's Wonka has worldly concerns and problems. The need to resolve his daddy issues becomes the point of the film. Book- and Wilder-Wonka remain the grown-up antagonists in their stories, while we follow

Inside Charlie's Chocolate Factory

Charlie as the protagonist, the heart of the story, all the way through. It is Charlie's (unwitting) progress towards his glorious chocolatey reward in which we invest, about which we care. Wilder's Wonka is, as in the book, the embellishment and excitement round the edges – his batty, barmy, nutty, screwy, dippy, dotty, daffy, goofy, beany, buggy, wacky, loony nature dazzling and drawing our attention but, narratively speaking, remaining decoration.

In the 2005 film, Wonka's life is the main event and both the emphasis on and the nature of his journey make his a very different story from Roald Dahl's – and very far removed, in fact, from the notion of family he demonstrates in all his books.

Roald's family – the one he was born into as a child and the one he created as a man – were everything to him, and his experience of the former in particular was idyllic. Perhaps it is only someone who has experienced first-hand what family can and should mean who can be so ruthless when they write about those who fall short of producing the ideal for their offspring. Blood family, to Roald

Johnny Depp as Willy Wonka.

Charlie and the Bucket family from the 2005 film.

Dahl the writer, means nothing by itself. What matters, always, is that the grown-ups in charge of the child put him or her first – not by indulging the child's every whim but in the ways that really matter: by protecting the naturally vulnerable offspring, by cultivating their strengths and curing or minimizing their weaknesses. Grandmotherhood alone, for example, won't save you, but being a good grandmother will have heroes effectively laying down their little mouse-lives for you, as in *The Witches*. Danny's father is a hero because he champions his son for all the world to see. The parents of the eponymous Matilda are contemptible because they do not, and in the same book Miss Trunchbull is not given a second chance when we find out she is Miss Honey's aunt. Her fate is sealed because she has treated her niece so badly. Matilda herself finds happiness with Miss Honey, the only adult – and complete non-relation – who sees and loves her for what she is. This fictional treatment of family is all of a piece with a man who in real life missed no opportunity to make things a bit more fun, a little bit more exciting or interesting for his

Inside Charlie's Chocolate Factory

children – from swearing that his recipe for bacon-and-marmalade-topped toast came from a young prince in Dar es Salaam after Roald had rescued him from a giant python (as his third daughter Ophelia recalls in *Memories with Food at Gipsy House*) to standing outside their bedroom windows at night, pretending to be a big friendly giant blowing dreams through their windows. The idea of a child (of whatever age) forgiving a bad parent, and the unthinkableness of a happy ending without it, is very modern and not one that has much to do with Roald's world view at all. It is idealistic and sentimental, and is more concerned with relieving adult anxieties (there is nothing we can do so bad that it cannot ultimately be undone) than entertaining child viewers/readers or slaking their thirst for natural justice.

Roald disliked Wilder's portrayal of Wonka. He had wanted Peter Sellers or Spike Milligan for the part and thought Wilder was completely wrong for the role, playing it 'for subtle adult laughs'. It seems a harsh judgement from the writer who consciously penned a book for children that would delight them without boring senseless the adults who had to read it aloud.

Stuart's analysis of what made his film work applies equally to the book: 'Each individual's traits are spelled out in broad strokes and are instantly recognizable, but the wit, the occasional absurdity in the writing and the superb portrayals [avoid the danger], as with all morality tales, of being pedantic.' It is possible that Roald was never able to look clearly at the film, so depressed was he by the adaptation experience as well as the difficulties he was having in writing what would eventually become *Charlie and the Great Glass Elevator* by the time the film came out.

It is after all the appeal to adults that first gave impetus to *Willy Wonka and the Chocolate Factory*'s second life on television, video and DVD, and that continues to make it popular and known to new generations today. It is not more famous than the book – as the *Mary Poppins* film has become, doubtless causing P. L. Travers to weep ever louder in her grave – but the 1971 film is surely at least as familiar and may even, these days, bring more people to the book for the first time than word-of-mouth recommendations from other readers do.

NEXT SPREAD:
A scene from the 2005 film:
Willy Wonka and the parents
and children watch in shock
as Augustus Gloop ascends
the chocolate chute.

Inside Charlie's Chocolate Factory

On the Stage

So that's *Charlie*, star of the screen. But what of *Charlie* – cue the roar of the greasepaint, the smell of the crowd – star of the stage?

In 2008 Warner Bros, who held the stage rights to *Charlie*, approached Sam Mendes's company, Neal Street Productions, to ask if they wanted to partner with them and make the book into a musical. Mendes and his fellow producers Caro Newling and Pippa Harris agreed and over the next couple of years they and Warner Bros put together what Newling calls the 'creative army', including all the usual vast panoply of designers of costumes, sets, lighting and so on, a choreographer, scriptwriter, composer and lyricist, and on top of that such exotic fare as a video and projection designer, and puppet and illusion creator, with whom primary responsibility for such challenges as bringing the Oompa-Loompas and team of trained squirrels to life would rest.

At first Mendes had planned only to be one of the show's executive

ABOVE: Sam Mendes (rear left), Douglas Hodge (rear right) and Charlie actors Jack Costello, Tom Klenerman, Louis Suc and Isaac Rouse at an after-party, celebrating the press-night performance of *Charlie and the Chocolate Factory*.

OPPOSITE: Douglas Hodge as Willy Wonka in the musical.

The press and children arrive at the Wonka factory gates.

producers, but when the first script and songs started to come in he could resist no longer and became the musical's director. By the time rehearsals began in 2013, he had only just finished directing the new James Bond film *Skyfall*. 'It was probably not the most sensible thing to do, to follow the biggest movie I've ever done with the biggest show,' he told a team of documentary-makers who were filming him at the time, but that was how the timetable had worked out. So it was on with the (massive, multimillion-dollar, using-sixty-tons-of-machinery-so-the-theatre-ceiling-had-to-be-reinforced-with-steel) show.

Douglas Hodge, an actor who was best known for serious dramatic theatre roles but who had also won a Tony Award for *La Cage aux Folles* on Broadway in 2010 was cast as Willy Wonka. He compiled a scrapbook of pictures of people like Michael Jackson, David Bowie, Salvador Dali, Mick Jagger, Prince and Charlie Chaplin, whose strange lives or idiosyncratic looks gave him some inspiration when it came to creating his version of Wonka. Hodge admired Wilder's

Inside Charlie's Chocolate Factory

performance but didn't want to reproduce it – for practical as well as artistic reasons. 'I'm working in a different medium,' he says. 'I really admire Gene Wilder's version, but his energy – that druggy, transcendental, gently enigmatic thing– is different from what I require to sing huge songs and fill a theatre full of children. There's a different engine powering a big West End musical.'

Casting Charlie and the rest of the Golden Ticket winners took nine months. Like Mel Stuart, the casting directors looked at but also beyond stage-school students for auditionees. Employment rules for children meant that they needed three or four young actors for each of the juvenile roles. They held hundreds of auditions, looking for frenetically active, kinetic boys for Mike Teavee, Augustuses who were comfortable playing overweight characters, Violets who could play a child rap and R&B star, and Verucas who either had or would quickly pick up in training the ballet moves her princessy character would need. The Charlie actors didn't need to dance much; they only had to have good singing voices and be able to hold the attention of a

Mya Olaye as Violet Beauregarde, and Tom Klenerman as Charlie.

The Oompa-Loompas: part actors, part hand-puppets.

Jack Costello as Charlie, at the rubbish dump.

2,200-strong audience in the West End during almost every scene in a two-and-a-half-hour show.

Incredibly, the casting directors found them all and rehearsals started in earnest as juggernauts containing the sets, and all the hand-made machinery needed to make them work, began arriving at the Theatre Royal, London.

'It was a complete joy to do,' says Newling now. 'Mainly because everyone had loved *Charlie* in childhood. And the one or two who hadn't read the book soon did and became completely hooked. Of course we had a phenomenal amount of talent in our cast and crew, but in the end it was their response to *Charlie* that really made it work.'

The show opened in June 2013 and continues to play to packed houses every night, full of children – and their parents – eagerly waiting to see their adored characters come to life.

'They're wildly disappointed to see me in real life if they come round to the stage door,' says Hodge. 'I wish I could stay in costume. It's wonderful how entranced they still are by the magic. That's what you love.'

The Opera

The putting together of film, theatrical or almost any other kind of adaptation is all a long way from the experience of book-writing. Roald Dahl once described it as a lonely profession with one great compensation: as soon as you were holed up alone in your writing hut with just your pencils and your paper, you had 'total and absolute freedom' to get on with it.

The operatic adaptation of *Charlie and the Chocolate Factory* had an even longer gestation than the musical. The idea was first mooted in 1997 but it wasn't until thirteen years later – after a convoluted rights wrangle and many attempts to secure funding, on top of all the creative work involved in writing, composing and workshopping the actual piece – that composer Peter Ash and writer (and biographer of Roald Dahl) Donald Sturrock actually saw their work premiere. *The Golden Ticket* opened at the Opera Theatre of Saint Louis in Missouri, USA, in a co-production with Ireland's Wexford Festival Opera (where it would receive its European premiere) and the American Lyric Theater in June 2010.

Inside Charlie's Chocolate Factory

It had originally been called *Charlie and the Chocolate Factory* but that, Sturrock ruefully recalls, turned out to be a marketing mistake when there was a preview performance of the score at the Bridgewater Hall in Manchester, England. 'We said quite clearly on the posters that it was a concert performance. But nevertheless a lot of people turned up expecting a stage version of the Gene Wilder film. There was quite an exodus at the interval, and requests for refunds!'

But once *The Golden Ticket* was performed for an audience who understood what they had bought tickets for, the opera received a rapturous reception.

It was a production designed to introduce children to opera. The music contained hints of everything and everyone from Wagner to Britten and – like its source material – was full of apposite jokes that would appeal to adults and that the children could appreciate later. For example, the first sight of the chocolate river accompanied by music echoes *Das Rheingold*, the first of Wagner's *Ring* cycle, set around the Rhine river, which flows from the Swiss Alps (much like Switzerland's famous milk chocolate, of course) through Germany and on through the Netherlands before finally coming out into the Fudge Room. I'm sorry, I mean the North Sea. And after a reference to Turkish Delight in *The Golden Ticket*'s Nut Room there is a blast of Turkish janissary music – though the connection might take a child in the audience even longer to understand than the whole square-sweets-that-look-round thing.

Happiest of all was the discovery Sturrock had made that the four 'bad' children in the book fitted rather neatly into various operatic stereotypes. Augustus Gloop was a shoo-in as a fat Italian tenor, given to breaking into Puccini-esque arias at moments of high emotion – falling into the river, say – while shrill show-off Violet became a coloratura soprano (traditionally the most – um – high-maintenance of operatic performers, the one producing the vocal runs and leaps that cause uninitiated German emperors to complain of too many notes. For *The Golden Ticket*, imagine Nellie Melba ululating round a wad of gum – there you go). Veruca Salt was clearly a mezzo-soprano, the deeper, more assertive voice conveying Veruca's perennially imperative mood. And, rounding things off, Mike Teavee's jittering, gun-toting hyperactivity found perfect expression as a baroque-style counter-tenor, full of Monteverdian agitation.

OPPOSITE: Daniel Okulitch starred as Willy Wonka and Michael Kepler Meo played the role of Charlie in *The Golden Ticket* opera.

Bringing the Characters to Life

It is interesting and edifying to see how easily the book's characters can
have their flaws updated or modulated according to the needs of the
new form or age in which they find themselves. Mike Teavee's
obsessions can be mapped on to whatever the current parental bugbear
is. As time has gone on it has morphed from guns and television to the
internet and violent video games (in the 2005 film and the latest stage
musical), but if you chose to set the story in another era it could just as
well be anything from Tamagotchis to fishing in the creek for sprats –
anything that a child prefers to be doing rather than sitting quietly with
a book as parents would like. In Burton's film, Violet's competitiveness
(and the source of it, her parents) translated perfectly into the kind of
dead-eyed mother–daughter team that exists in every school and whose
dedication to winning every trophy going is due not to a noble
Corinthian spirit but to a perverse and indefatigable acquisitive instinct,
while in the stage musical she translates seamlessly into a child star,
with the same furious need to chomp and stomp on all her competitors.

The ease with which Roald Dahl's characters can be updated is
another sign that what he created is in essence a fairy tale – eternal
truths, dangers, human weaknesses embodied in a handful of characters

Inside Charlie's Chocolate Factory

(or caricatures) and put into a story that will lay them all bare.

Nevertheless, there was still the odd structure of the novel to contend with, as noted by David Greig, writer of the stage musical, who says:

> *I had a wonderful conversation once with Dennis Kelly when he was writing [the script for] Matilda [the musical]. And he said, 'D'you know, I hate Roald Dahl. Because he just made it up!' By which he meant that Dahl was telling his story night by night, so he didn't need to know where he was going when he started, as long as it held together moment by moment . . . But you realize as you work on it [for a different medium] that there's a reason traditional narrative structure exists – it will carry you through a two-hour show without dropping you.*

Of course this is not the whole truth – we know that *Charlie*, like most of Roald Dahl's and indeed most authors' books, went through a rigorous editing process. But it does capture part of the truth, perhaps, of the book's continuous and continuing appeal: that it retains the sense of spontaneity, the rush of imagination that buoys readers and carries them

In the UK, *Charlie and the Chocolate Factory* was adapted for stage in the s by Jeremy Raison. It received much acclaim and toured for ten years, nationally and internationally.

along in print just as it must have carried Roald and his children from bedtime to bedtime.

The first-ever theatrical adaptation of *Charlie and the Chocolate Factory* was by an elementary-school teacher called Richard R. George in New York, in 1975. He turned the book into a play for his sixth-grade students and then wrote to Roald Dahl to see if it could be published so that students in other schools could enjoy it too. Roald said it could, and so it was. George dealt with the structural problems of the book by simply having a narrator come on, whizz through chunks of text and then dash off again. Which is, of course, a swift and sure way to keep your young actors and parental audience on track, but both Sturrock and Greig required something a bit more sophisticated for their productions.

They each chose to condense the book's introduction to the characters (by zapping through television interviews with the winners and not drawing out Charlie's disappointments for such an agonizingly long time). And they both felt that because it's more difficult for a child in the audience to put himself in the shoes of a flesh-and-blood figure in front of him or her than it is for a reader to do so in a written story, they needed to humanize Charlie and to establish something about him and his relationship with Willy Wonka that would make his inheritance of the factory more than a simple matter of chance or a reward, as Greig puts it, 'simply for not being bad'.

Sturrock gave Charlie an aria to sing as he dishes up the evening's cabbage-soup supper,

Inside Charlie's Chocolate Factory

about his worries for his grandparents, and both he and Grieg added a sense of Charlie's life outside the home. Sturrock introduced a sweet-shop owner and Greig a tramp who lives near the dump beside Charlie's house, each of whom knows Charlie and appreciates him as a little boy with a good heart and a vivid imagination, who deserves the chance to express himself.

In the opera, Charlie invents new sweets with the shop owner, and in the musical the tramp watches him pick over new leavings at the dump to see if anything can be pressed into service back home. Tramp and shop owner are both Wonka in disguise, which makes Charlie's good fortune at the end better earned than it is in the book and, in an oblique way, restores some of the emotional detail and pull of the reading experience that is lost when the printed page is realized on stage or screen.

But why adapt *Charlie* – for stage, for screen or for anything else? Why take on the problems of such a book and the wild expectations of the child in the audience who is in the throes of passionate Dahl-adoration, along with an accompanying parental audience probably equally desperate to be transported back to their own heady childhood when anything could happen and, in a certain writer's hands, probably would?

It seems all the writers and directors were drawn to the duality of the book. The gorgeous, fantastical confection is uppermost (and works like catnip on set designers, effects creators and anyone who knows that, given the chance, they have the ability to bring that Chocolate Room, those squirrels, that boiled-sweet boat to life) and the murky adult undercurrents run underneath. That is what, after all, keeps us coming back to fairy tales. All those who have worked on versions of *Charlie* say something along these lines, but Greig perhaps puts it best:

> *No matter how long it went on, no matter how many times I had to re-write, or go back, no matter how many times the process maddened me, it was genuinely a pleasure working on it. It's juicy and meaty – I think with* Charlie, *Dahl tapped into something quite profound. You get lucky as a writer if you do that once a lifetime, and I think Dahl did it more than once.*

Perhaps, however, there is also another reason. Mel Stuart did it, basically, for his daughter. Sturrock did it to introduce children to experiences that might otherwise elude them. Burton did it for the same reason he seems to make most of his films – for the child within us all. Again, Greig perhaps puts it best:

> *My touchstone for the whole thing was an eight-year-old boy in the audience – the age my son was when I started work on it. I don't really care what anyone else thinks. That eight-year-old might never have been to the theatre before – certainly it's very likely he won't have been before or go again that year. His family have paid lots of money for their tickets because they want him to have an amazing time. I kept picturing him in Row 43. He's probably already read the book. He probably has bits he particularly loved and would be disappointed not to see in the show. So it's very, very important to stick closely to the book. For children, it's almost like a religious ritual and the story is a parable – you can't just miss a step, take a shortcut. So all the way through the process I tried to keep that kid in my mind and honour his experience. It was so important that he be surprised – but also that he have every moment he knew confirmed.*

Entertainment first – let the experience work as it will thereafter. That was Roald Dahl's writing philosophy. We will of course never know what he would have thought of all the adaptations of *Charlie* since the 1971 film, or of the ones that will doubtless emerge in years to come. But the animating instinct of the creators of the adaptations was essentially the same as Roald Dahl's own – and we hope that pleases the shade of a tall, mercurial man standing beneath a tree, blowing dreams into the air.

WILLIE WONKA
THE GOLDEN TICKET

AUGUSTUS GLOOP
VISITS THE FACTORY
THE GOLDEN TICKET

THE OOMP-LOOMPAS
THE GOLDEN TICKET

VIOLET BECOMES A
BLUEBERRY

Costume designs
from *The Golden
Ticket* opera,
designed by the late
Tony Award winner
Martin Pakledinaz.

BEHIND THE GATES OF
THE CHOCOLATE FACTORY
A Visual Tour

PREVIOUS SPREAD:
Quentin Blake's
depiction of the Golden
Ticket holders as they
enter Willy Wonka's
chocolate factory.

Introduction

In 1962, when the time came to start thinking about possible illustrators for *Charlie and the Chocolate Factory*, Roald Dahl's first choice was a young man called Maurice Sendak, whose drawings for Robert Graves's *The Big Green Book* he had much enjoyed. (Graves's tale is about an orphan called Jack who uses a book of spells he finds in the attic to get his own back on the unforgivably boring aunt and uncle he lives with – a story whose instincts have much common ground with both Roald Dahl and Maurice Sendak.) It's an even more alluring what-if situation than the prospect of Spike Milligan or Peter Sellers playing Willy Wonka, but Sendak was unavailable. The timing suggests he was probably working on the book that would make him famous, *Where the Wild Things Are*, which came out in 1963.

Although he didn't get his first choice back then, Roald Dahl has always been well-served by his illustrators, from the very first (Sendak's loss was Joseph Schindelman's gain) to the last (so far), Quentin Blake – a man whose sensibilities fit so beautifully and whose association with Roald Dahl is so strong that it is impossible to envisage it not somehow going on forever.

Here – in the company of several different interpretations of Willy Wonka, Charlie and of fellow Golden Ticket holders – is a tour of *Charlie and the Chocolate Factory* as visualized by the book's illustrators and those charged with bringing Roald Dahl's creations to life on both stage and screen over the years.

In the words of Mr Willy Wonka . . . Will you please hang your coats and hats on those pegs over here, and then follow me. *That's* the way! Good! Everyone ready? Come on, then! Here we go!

RIGHT: Willy Wonka welcoming Charlie to his chocolate factory, illustrated by Quentin Blake.

Inside Charlie's Chocolate Factory

Joseph Schindelman

*'I wanted to retain that sense of innocence in
Charlie . . . He was poor and he looked it '*
– Joseph Schindelman

The first person to illustrate *Charlie and the Chocolate Factory* was
American artist Joseph Schindelman. He only received the manuscript
once he had already accepted the job of illustrating the book. More
than four decades later, he told Roald Dahl's grandson Luke Kelly that
the story had been described to him 'as a children's book about some
wilful children and one child who deserved better than he had at the
moment; and it was almost a morality story. I was thinking of the seven
sins – you know, gluttony – and I liked it'.

He thought the book was brilliant. 'I was put in mind of Cruikshank
and Dickens – that era felt right in terms of how this story played out.'
He used a very fine ink pen so that he could make the characters and
scenes as detailed as possible. 'There was a rightness about it, an
innocence.' When he provided the publisher with the first sketches they
didn't ask for any changes (though he had done so many pictures that
they weren't able to use them all in the book).

Both author and illustrator seemed to be on the same wavelength
from the beginning. They first met at the publisher's offices. Roald didn't
say much about the drawings – Schindelman thinks it might have been
because he had wanted to choose his own illustrator but had not been
allowed – but afterwards they took a walk together and talked politics
rather than books or art 'and I enjoyed it because it was left wing and
very liberal, and I approved!' Schindelman remembered. 'We didn't
solve the problems of the world . . . It wasn't a very long walk.' He came
away further appreciating what Roald Dahl had written and his
imagination and sense of humour. But of course, like any artist – 'I wish
he had said he liked the drawings.'

'I'm elated to be part of this legacy. It's totally unexpected for me. I
mean, the success is really overwhelming, and I appreciate it. I've always
been impressed with the book, the writing, the imagination, the colour,
descriptions. I still love the book.'

Joseph Schindelman's cover
for the original edition
(Knopf, 1964).

Faith Jaques's cover for the first UK paperback edition (Puffin, 1973).

Faith Jaques

Just as each generation has its James Bond or Sherlock Holmes as a standard from which all others deviate, regardless of actual chronology or accuracy, so we all have 'our' editions of children's books. When it comes to *Charlie*, the late Faith Jaques's is mine (and most other thirty-somethings'). When I later discovered that she was a compulsive reader who loved to be alone and kept cats because they are the only pets that allow you to be both, my adoration of Jaques and her work could only increase.

Jaques's illustrations are – perhaps even more than Schindelman's – incredibly detailed and intricate drawings.

'I like to know how chairs and tables are made, how a building is constructed,' she once said. 'I like to have as much knowledge and information as possible, in order to select the important factors and throw out what's unnecessary. It's an imaginative and analytical process all in one.'

To keep herself supplied with such information (in the days before the internet, children), she built up a personal library and an archive of over 15,000 pictures on the history of costume, social history, the natural world, architecture, ornamentation and much more, and she honed her skills for distilling the essence of a scene or situation into a telling picture during her years producing advertisements for everyone from the Gas Board to Fortnum and Mason.

All this – her approach, her skill, her knowledge – is what gives us in Jaques's chocolate factory a gum machine (black and white inside the book, but in full, glorious colour on the cover) that looks as though it might actually work, if you only had the chance to build it – *if only!* – or perhaps if you just stared long enough and willed it hard enough into being. Her Inventing Room looks like a viable laboratory and her squirrels the very essence of . . . squirrelity. In fact, if you'll just excuse me, I'm just going to look at that gum machine again. I'm older now – I bet my will is stronger than it was back then . . .

Inside Charlie's Chocolate Factory

Michael Foreman

'I was a great admirer of Dahl's books and stories for adults,' says *Charlie*'s third illustrator, Michael Foreman, 'and my New York publisher had tried to put us together when he began writing for younger people but it didn't happen until much later, when they wanted to give Charlie a fresh look and I took over from Faith Jaques.'

By that time, in 1985, Foreman had been an illustrator of children's books for over twenty years, had won the first of his two Kate Greenaway medals and been nominated for the international Hans Christian Andersen Award (which he would win in 2010). 'I had one meeting with Roald Dahl, in a restaurant on the King's Road,' he says. 'I don't remember him giving me any direction – I just went away and did the drawings. I knew they had to be black and white, so that immediately meant pen and ink, and I used cross-hatching rather than a lot of wash because I wanted them crisp and clear, not too dark.'

Michael Foreman's cover for the second UK paperback edition (Puffin, 1985).

As well as the characters, he says, the machinery really appealed to him: 'I envisaged Victorian stuff – lots of reels, cogs and pipework. Lots of shiny stuff.'

The only thing Roald Dahl didn't like when he got the drawings, Foreman says, was his take on Willy Wonka. 'I had thought that if I were the owner of a chocolate factory like that, I would be eating too much of the product all day long – so I made him tubby! So that I had to change.'

Quentin Blake's latest cover
(Puffin, 2013).

Quentin Blake

When Quentin Blake was suggested as an illustrator to Roald Dahl
(for his book for younger readers, *The Enormous Crocodile*), Roald
at first wondered whether he needed someone with a less distinctive
style. But soon it became clear that Blake's gleeful, literally spiky,
endlessly energetic drawings were the perfect complement to Roald
Dahl's gleeful, metaphorically spiky and endlessly energetic prose,
and they have worked in harmony together ever since.

'At first, with *The Enormous Crocodile* and *The Twits*, we didn't
communicate as much directly as we did later,' he says. 'We did it
mostly through our publishers and letters. I remember him writing to
tell me that Mr Twit's beard should stick out more at the sides. *The
BFG* was when we really began to talk to each other much more.'
There was much discussion in particular about what the BFG should
wear. He sported an apron at first, 'but it kept getting in the way',
recalls Blake – and they couldn't decide what he should wear on his
feet. A few days later, Blake received in the post one of Roald's own
battered, Norwegian-style leather sandals, and the problem was
solved.

'Curiously enough,' says Quentin Blake, '*Charlie and the
Chocolate Factory* was the first book I illustrated after Dahl died.
Puffin wanted me to re-illustrate the books that he had written
before our collaboration had begun. I couldn't consult him, but I sort
of felt that I knew how he would feel about it all. And I remembered
talking to him once about how lively and nervous a person Willy
Wonka was, jumping about all the time. And of course I could talk to
Liccy [Roald's widow]. With most of the characters it was fairly
obvious what to do but I wanted to rethink the Oompa-Loompas by
having their hair stand on end, and she said Roald would have
approved. I wanted to make them into more of a part of Wonka's
team, not employees or slaves but people as naughty as he is – which
they are, in the book.'

Over the years, he had seen all the earlier illustrators' versions –
'all rather good' – but didn't go back to refresh his memory before he
began his own. 'Willy Wonka was interesting – I think I made his

Inside Charlie's Chocolate Factory

bow tie bigger than anyone else had. And tails on coats are always good because they show when people are moving – they fly out!' And in contrast (we must infer) to Jaques's work, he enjoyed 'inventing' the machines because 'I wanted to make them look eccentric – as if they either wouldn't work, or would only work in very strange ways'.

What was always good about working with Roald Dahl, he says, was that no two books were the same. 'Manuscripts would come and you would think, What has he done now? So although Charlie had already existed, when I was "inside the factory" it was almost like doing an entirely new book for me.'

Most of all, Blake remembers that Roald was an author keen always to have as many pictures in his books as possible, to make it as fulfilling an experience as possible for children.

'The text wasn't sacred. If something could be changed to make the book more complete, he wanted to do it. He was willing to change things if he thought it would be better for his readers.'

Quentin Blake and Roald Dahl, looking at the artwork for *The Witches*.

Self-portrait with Roald Dahl, by Quentin Blake.

Willy Wonka

'When you think about it,' said Joseph Schindelman, 'he is so well described by Roald Dahl that you almost couldn't miss. I mean, it was like taking a photograph.'

Director Tim Burton felt that 'it's sort of abstract and leaves room for interpretation too . . . There's a certain kind of elegance to the character that's described and that you kind of want to retain . . . He lives in his own world, so he's not necessarily completely contemporary, not hip to the jive.'

Joseph Schindelman.   Faith Jaques.

Inside Charlie's Chocolate Factory

'[Mr Wonka's] eyes were most marvellously bright. They seemed to be sparkling and twinkling at you all the time. The whole face, in fact, was alight with fun and laughter.'

'He's barmy! He's nutty! He's screwy! He's batty! He's dippy! He's dotty! He's daffy! He's goofy! He's beany! He's buggy! He's wacky! He's loony!'

Michael Foreman.

Quentin Blake.

Charlie Bucket

'The one thing he longed for more than anything else was . . . CHOCOLATE.'

TOP LEFT:
Joseph Schindelman.

TOP RIGHT:
Faith Jaques.

BOTTOM LEFT:
Michael Foreman.

BOTTOM RIGHT:
Quentin Blake.

Inside Charlie's Chocolate Factory

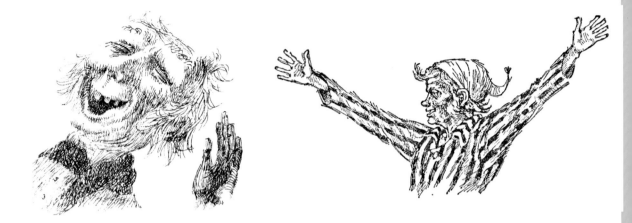

Grandpa Joe

'He was ninety-six and a half, and that is just about as old as anybody can be.'

TOP LEFT:
Joseph Schindelman.

TOP RIGHT:
Faith Jaques.

BOTTOM LEFT:
Michael Foreman.

BOTTOM RIGHT:
Quentin Blake.

Veruca Salt

'[Her father] gives her anything she wants! Absolutely anything!!'

TOP LEFT:
Joseph Schindelman.

TOP RIGHT:
Faith Jaques.

BOTTOM LEFT:
Michael Foreman.

BOTTOM RIGHT:
Quentin Blake.

Inside Charlie's Chocolate Factory

Violet Beauregarde

*'My mother says it's not ladylike and looks ugly to see a girl's jaws going up
and down like mine do all the time, but I don't agree.'*

TOP LEFT:
Faith Jaques.

TOP RIGHT:
Joseph Schindelman.

BOTTOM LEFT:
Michael Foreman.

BOTTOM RIGHT:
Quentin Blake.

Augustus Gloop

'Eating is his hobby, you know. That's all he's *interested in.'*

TOP (LEFT TO RIGHT):
Joseph Schindelman and Faith Jaques.

BOTTOM (LEFT TO RIGHT):
Michael Foreman and Quentin Blake.

Inside Charlie's Chocolate Factory

Mike Teavee

'He must be crazy! Look at all those toy pistols he's got hanging all over him!'

TOP LEFT:
Joseph Schindelman.

TOP RIGHT:
Faith Jaques.

BOTTOM LEFT:
Michael Foreman.

BOTTOM RIGHT:
Quentin Blake.

The Oompa-Loompas
'... *they were no larger than medium-sized dolls* ...'

TOP:
Joseph Schindelman.

BOTTOM:
Michael Foreman.

Inside Charlie's Chocolate Factory

'They are wonderful workers . . . They love dancing and music. They are always making up songs . . . I must warn you, though, that they are rather mischievous. They like jokes.'

Schindelman's illustration of Charlie at the factory gates.

'Welcome to the factory!'

'The illustration of the gate was just a fabrication. I did some lettering-type design. I had studied ornate design going back in history, and it sort of just fell into place and felt right' – Joseph Schindelman

For the paperback edition of the book, Schindelman extended the factory from the front cover to the back. 'There were a lot more barrels and pipes and little buildings and passageways – not that I got it all in but I felt that it should be a lot more colourful than the first version. The first version was simply the chocolate bar and the [title] lettering that sort of moved into the gate as well.'

For the 2005 film, Burton wanted 'a building with a Hoover Dam-like optimism and strength, but then once it gets dark looks slightly foreboding' to contrast with the intricacy and busyness of the candy-making operations inside. Like set and costume designer Mark Thompson, who took English artist L. S. Lowry as one of his inspirations when creating the exterior sets for the latest stage musical, Burton wanted to show a timeless but still gritty, realistic-looking environment. Alex McDowell, the film's designer, scouted various industrial mill towns in the north of England but 'a real place was never going to be stylized enough for Tim, so it was back to the Pinewood backlot to start building something that looked grim, wet and depressing on the outside but transitioned believably into a magical kingdom inside.' The Oompa-Loompas were the answer. 'They brought their own aesthetic,' laughed McDowell, 'and have just run riot in there.'

Inside Charlie's Chocolate Factory

'In the town itself, actually within sight of the house in which Charlie lived, there was an ENORMOUS CHOCOLATE FACTORY! . . . It was the largest and most famous in the whole world! It was WONKA'S FACTORY . . . It had huge iron gates leading into it, and a high wall surrounding it, and smoke belching from its chimneys, and strange whizzing sounds coming from deep inside it. And outside the walls, for half a mile around in every direction, the air was scented with the heavy rich smell of melting chocolate!'

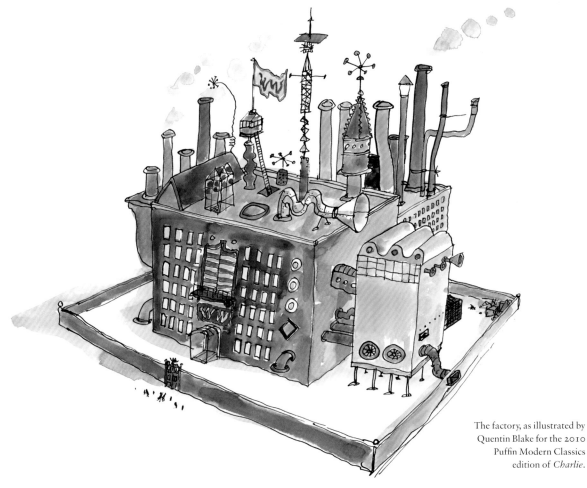

The factory, as illustrated by Quentin Blake for the 2010 Puffin Modern Classics edition of *Charlie*.

The chocolate river and its banks,
illustrated by Joseph Schindelman (ABOVE)
and Faith Jaques (BELOW).

The Chocolate Room

As with Wonka, the Chocolate Room is described in such loving and intricate detail that most of the decision-making is taken out of the illustrator's hands. The main challenge, Joseph Schindelman remembers, was where to place the waterfall and extend the river so that it could carry the boat off later on.

Some reviewers expressed disappointment at the absence of the chocolate river and boat ride from the musical production of *Charlie*, and with the production's rendering of the waterfall as a narrow strip of brown and gold-lit wavy tubes coming down from the flies. 'Like a giant Curly Wurly,' sniffed one reviewer – so, even if the waterfall was underwhelming, at least you could argue that it was apposite. But it proved too difficult to create the necessary effects within a live show and still get the production to come in at anything like a reasonable running time. There is nothing like having to assemble and dismantle a foaming cataract of chocolate to stop your show dead in its tracks.

Inside Charlie's Chocolate Factory

'I am a bit sad that we lost the river and the boat,' says Thompson (although the boat does appear in a later scene). But care and attention was lavished on every remaining detail. Thompson can be seen in a documentary film about the making of musicals staring in dismay at a 'too flat, vulgar' flower decorating the Chocolate Room set. 'That's not edible,' he says, fixing it with a gimlet eye, and speaking metaphorically (as it wasn't one of those parts of the set that was designed to be eaten). 'It's got no flavour.'

Later on he requests that the squirrels' eyes be made brighter. 'They need crazed, drug-filled-weekend eyes,' he explains. And, once he says it, you know what he means. That's exactly how squirrels look and that's exactly why Roald Dahl was so right to use them in his story. There's menacing madness in those shiny black stares.

On the set of the 1971 film, the size of the Chocolate Room caused many lighting problems for Mel Stuart and his crew, the chocolate waterfall broke down on more than one occasion, and the filming of the boat trip took just about forever – but the generations of viewers who went on to enjoy their efforts have made them all worthwhile.

For the 2005 production designer Alex McDowell, as for most of those

The chocolate waterfall as depicted by Michael Foreman (ABOVE) and Quentin Blake (BELOW).

The Oompa-Loompas in the Chocolate Room: Tim Burton's
sketch (ABOVE) and the actual realization on film (BELOW AND OPPOSITE).

who have attempted to adapt the book, the Chocolate Room was the main challenge: 'How do you create a place that is described like Disneyland that is scary as well but also appealing to children – all of which was central to Tim [Burton]'s take on Wonka's character? It's a really interesting problem, visually – to tone down the brightness and theme-parkishness and have a place that might eat as well as feed small children . . .'

It was a process that began with small watercolour sketches (a further selection can be seen on pages 72–73) that Burton frequently draws to hone and communicate to others his ideas for sets, characters and costumes in his films, and it led to old-fashioned storyboarding, practice builds and simulated sets created with design-visualization software. The latter was particularly useful for a film that demanded early commitment to exactly where to place the required thirty-foot-high steel and fibreglass trees. Then final adjustments were made to resolve practical problems, such as the limited space in which cameras could manoeuvre around the sets (which meant that the more that

Inside Charlie's Chocolate Factory

could be shot from the side, the better); and the different camera-angle modifications that were needed to make certain shots of Oompa-Loompa Deep Roy look believable. All these issues became apparent once the sets were finalized and the build was beginning.

McDowell wanted to give the impression of a room whose ground had been mined for its delicious chocolatey content, so they built it around the idea of a landscape that had been dug and turned over as if by an ice-cream scoop (the rounded, spherical and half-spherical shapes involved were deliberately echoed throughout the film – the spherical Nut Room, for example, and the circular doorways).

Schindelman said that film versions of the Chocolate Room usually made him smile. 'Hollywood takes liberties, shall we say! . . . Everything is altered and while it's fun to look at it doesn't have the flavour of what I think the drawings try to project. Everything's enhanced and babyish – overdone, but that's what Hollywood does: they overdo!'

> 'This is the nerve centre of the whole factory, the heart of the whole business! . . . And so beautiful!'

> '. . . there was a tremendous waterfall halfway along the river – a steep cliff over which the water curled and rolled in a solid sheet, and then went crashing down into a boiling churning whirlpool of froth and spray.'

The Boat

The SS *Wonkatania*, as it was called in the 1971 film, was originally conceived as a sixteenth-century three-masted sailboat. Alas, it couldn't fit on the set and had to be redesigned.

As part of film director Mel Stuart's efforts to evoke wherever possible the potential darkness in Wonka's character, the boat was made with only nine seats – suggesting that the factory owner knew one of his charges would no longer be with him by this point.

> *'It was a large open row boat with a tall front and a tall back (like a Viking boat of old), and it was of such a shining sparkling glistening pink colour that the whole thing looked as though it were made of bright, pink glass. There were many oars on either side of it, and as the boat came closer, the watchers on the riverbank could see that the oars were being pulled by masses of Oompa-Loompas – at least ten of them to each oar.'*

The SS *Wonkatania* from the 1971 film.

Inside Charlie's Chocolate Factory

'I made her by hollowing out an enormous boiled sweet!
Isn't she beautiful!'

TOP (FROM LEFT TO RIGHT):
Joseph Schindelman and Faith Jaques.

BOTTOM (FROM LEFT TO RIGHT):
Michael Foreman and Quentin Blake.

The Inventing Room

The Inventing Room was the only set over which Mel Stuart and his set designer Harper Goff disagreed. Stuart wanted the Inventing Room to have a Rube Goldberg–Heath Robinson-esque quality to it so that it would look weird and wonderful, but also as if it just might work. (In the stage musical, Mark Thompson enlisted the same quality for the contraptions the Bucket family use, made out of bits that Charlie scavenges from the dump – using the imagination that is soon to lift him out of this life and into the magical world of the factory forever.)

Goff had envisaged it as a hymn to modernity – all stainless-steel assembly lines and sleek efficiency. 'He stomped off the set in a snit,' says Stuart in *Pure Imagination*. 'But he returned a day later with a concept that was a perfect solution to the problem; a room with overtones of a junkyard.' Led by the film's construction manager Hank Wynands, the crew scoured Munich's bakeries, car dealerships and of

The Inventing Room, from the 1971 film.

Inside Charlie's Chocolate Factory

course junkyards for discarded bits of machinery that could be pressed into active – or at least active-looking – service. Tim Burton's people would go on a similar hunt when creating their Inventing Room; it includes scrap aeronautical parts and redundant confectionery factory machinery as well as trusty old car parts.

The gum machine appears to have seized the imagination of every illustrator, publisher, set designer and director – apart from, initially, Goff, who originally planned it as an enclosed entity. When he saw it, Stuart asked Goff to find a way of making it more visually interesting, and so he added the beehive (providing honey), boxing gloves (for pounding flour) and the tomato-squasher (for – well, you get the drift). You can understand its appeal. There's just something so inherently tempting – and funny – about all that effort, all that energy, all those ingredients being poured into the production of something so small and apparently ordinary as a strip of gum. It's like a metaphor for life, isn't it? No? I'm sorry, you're mumbling – I can't hear you. Onward!

The Inventing Room, from the 2005 film.

The Inventing Room

*'This is the most important
room in the entire factory! . . .
All my most secret new
inventions are cooking and
simmering in here!'*

*'The place was like
a witch's kitchen!'*

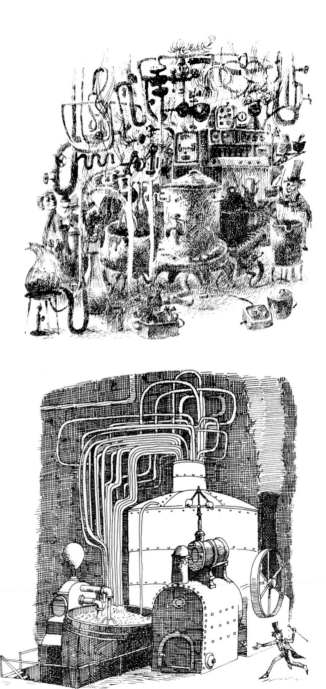

TOP:
Joseph Schindelman.

BOTTOM:
Michael Foreman.

Inside Charlie's Chocolate Factory

The Nut Room

The greatest problem for anyone trying to bring this room to life is of course the large number of trained (or realistically, movably fake) squirrels it requires to chuck bad nut Veruca down the chute. The problem, as we know, defeated Stuart, but special effects had moved on by the time Tim Burton was ready to transmute the pages into film, and the different possibilities offered by theatre allowed the musical's designer, director and choreographer to come up with a brilliant blend of puppetry and people to create the necessary nut-lovers.

According to Alex McDowell, 'the Nut Room was crazy. All the animatronic squirrels had to be incorporated into all of the seats and the centre was complicated because of the funnel in the ground – which had to be built in the air so that Veruca could fall down it. We built a lot of machinery that had to work – delivering nuts isn't easy.'

'It was an amazing sight. One hundred squirrels were seated upon high stools around a large table. On the table, there were mounds and mounds of walnuts, and the squirrels were all working away like mad, shelling the walnuts at a tremendous speed.'

The Nut Room,
from the 2005 film.

Inside Charlie's Chocolate Factory

The Television-Chocolate Room

When Mel Stuart first visited the all-white set, everything was so dazzling and the joins so neat that he couldn't find the door to let himself out. Hank Wynands took pity and showed him in the end.

'The room was painted white all over. Even the floor was white, and there wasn't a speck of dust anywhere. From the ceiling, huge lamps hung down and bathed the room in a brilliant blue-white light. The room was completely bare except at the far ends. At one of these ends there was an enormous camera on wheels, and a whole army of Oompa-Loompas was clustering around it . . .'

The Television-
Chocolate Room,
Faith Jaques.

Inside Charlie's Chocolate Factory

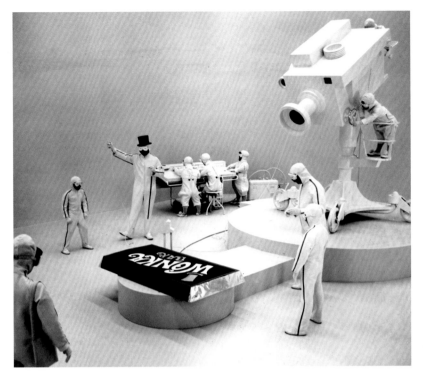

The Television-Chocolate Room,
from the 1971 film.

The Television-Chocolate Room,
from the 2005 film.

ABOVE:
The Great Glass Elevator, Michael Foreman.

OPPOSITE:
The Great Glass Elevator, from the 2005 film.

In the 1971 film, the Great Glass Elevator is renamed the Wonkavator and there were three versions built – a full-sized one for the actors' scenes, a three-foot-high one to film the breaking through the factory roof (which took twenty takes to get right) and a miniature one for the shots of it flying over the city.

The stage musical required such a new, complicated and temperamental piece of machinery to perform the effect of a glass lift flying through the air and across the stage with no visible means of support that Mark Thompson and the crew are still barely able to speak about it without collapsing under the strain of remembered horrors. But all was well on opening night, and has been ever since.

'This was the craziest lift he had ever seen. There were buttons everywhere! The walls, and even the ceiling, were covered all over with rows and rows and rows of small, black push buttons! There must have been a thousand of them on each wall, and another thousand on the ceiling!'

'This isn't just an ordinary up-and-down lift! . . . This lift can go sideways and longways and slantways and any other way you can think of! It can visit any single room in the whole factory, no matter where it is! You simply press the button . . . and zing! . . . you're off!'

Inside Charlie's Chocolate Factory

EVERLASTING GOBSTOPPERS
The Effect on Popular Culture

This LEGO® version of the
Chocolate Room was made by Nick
Franklin, a fan who owns an impressive
collection of *Charlie and the Chocolate
Factory* memorabilia. (See pages 140–141 for
more items from his collection.)

If you look closely, you can see swirling lollipops, the
Great Glass Elevator, Augustus Gloop stuck in the
chocolate tube and Willy Wonka, who was made with a
ring-master's face and other LEGO® pieces. The chocolate river
was created using a glue gun, with acrylic and gold paint applied
on top.

Inside Charlie's Chocolate Factory

Introduction

As we celebrate the fiftieth anniversary of *Charlie and the Chocolate Factory*, the story has obviously amply repaid the perceptive reviewers' early faith in it and even more amply put paid to others' dismissals. Not only does it still sell nearly half a million copies a year around the world, but references to it permeate popular culture as abundantly and apparently unstoppably as the smell of chocolate does the air of Wonka's factory.

Its very language has been adopted by our culture at large. 'Willy Wonka' is now shorthand for any kind of innovator or eccentric genius. The term has been used to describe everything from a British sweet-maker to a marijuana grower in Seattle and, at this very moment of typing, a Google alert has popped up to tell me that most recently a new manufacturer has been described as 'the Willy Wonka of 3D printing'. Having a Golden Ticket is synonymous with getting an access-all-areas pass to anything desirable. Most recently commentators were asking whether Twitter's IPO

was 'a Golden Ticket or all hype?'. It's the go-to theme of anyone setting up a competition, from the individual amateur (I have lost count of the number of children's parties I have been to as both child and parent where it was used in the games) to global brands. Tesco and Virgin have run Golden Ticket campaigns. Nestlé used it too when they launched one of their Wonka-brand ranges. As did – whisper (or Wispa) it – Cadbury, during the 2012 Olympics, offering seats at the Games to lucky winners. Of course, having a good seat at any of the most popular events at the Olympics was also referred to generally as having a Golden Ticket and, ironically, some of the security arrangements were criticized as 'handing a Golden Ticket to terrorists'. This was not

In 2009, Christopher Lloyd appeared in an online trailer for a fake horror film called *Gobstopper*, in which he plays a crazed Willy Wonka scaring teenagers visiting his chocolate factory.

PREVIOUS SPREAD: Collectible Kubrick™ figurines, inspired by the 2005 film. Made by Medicom Toy Corporation, Japan.

Russell Brand dressed as Willy Wonka
at the 2012 Olympics, London.

the only *Charlie* reference at the London 2012 Olympics as Russell Brand, arguably Britain's most famous eccentric, showed up at the closing ceremony in an outfit clearly channelling Willy Wonka. Singing 'Pure Imagination' – the best-known song from the 1971 film – to the thousands in the stadium and the millions worldwide watching from their homes, he summed up the mood of exuberant, wide-eyed wonder at all they had seen over the previous astonishing few weeks.

The language and the tropes of Roald Dahl's fifty-year-old book are now firmly embedded in our culture. Some of this can be attributed to the unusual and privileged position children's books hold in our lives. When *Charlie* was first published in 1964, you could still count on living a broadly similar lifestyle to your parents and peers, and on sharing a common body of knowledge – cultural, social, academic and whatever else. Since then, however, we have increasingly left behind collective experiences and replaced them with individualized ones. People's life journeys have changed dramatically. No longer

Inside Charlie's Chocolate Factory

resembling a conveyor-beltful of caramels passing at a steady clip in endless rows through an enrobing machine, to be packed neatly into boxes at the other end, life journeys have become more like bags of Maltesers being upended and skittering all over the floor to unpredictable resting places.

But children's lives in general have remained more uniform, and the experiences we share in childhood – the books we read, the TV programmes we watch and, indeed, the sweets we eat – later become rare moments of connection between strangers, and within and among generations. There's not a British thirty- or forty-something alive, for example, who hasn't had a tipsy conversation or two with a friend about the opening lines of *Bagpuss*, or the irreproducible thrill of one's first packet of Space Dust, while boggling over the fact that they can recall how candy cigarettes and cocoa-dusted coconut 'tobacco' used to be sold with blithe unconcern in every sweet shop in the land.

But it is our books that bind us most. They last longer than sweets, and withstand re-reading better than television withstands

In 2006, Charlie and the Chocolate Factory: The Ride opened at the Alton Towers theme park in Staffordshire, England. The eleven-minute experience features a boat ride along the chocolate river, during which passengers encounter characters from the book, and it ends with a flight-simulation trip in the Great Glass Elevator.

re-watching. We love them more passionately, and often we get a second bite at the cherry when we return to read them to our own children. In 2012, research by the University of Worcester found that *Charlie and the Chocolate Factory* was among the most common children's book adults had read – in a list with *Alice's Adventures in Wonderland*, *The Lion, the Witch and the Wardrobe* and *The Wind in the Willows*. Such a finding suggests this is not a book that people are ever going to abandon or forget.

Nick Franklin started his collection of *Charlie and the Chocolate Factory* memorabilia in 2005 after seeing the Tim Burton adaptation, but it was the 1971 film that sparked his interest in prop design, which is now his profession. He has close to a thousand items in his collection in Salford, England.

BELOW:
A Willy Wonka's Candy Factory Kit with original packaging, instructions, wrappers and mould.

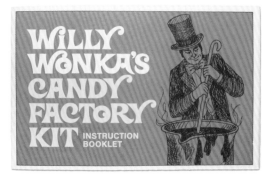

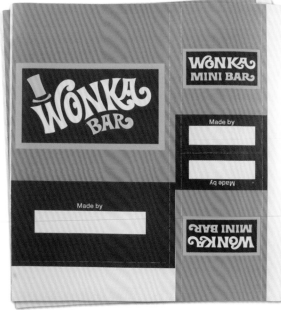

Inside Charlie's Chocolate Factory

This Golden Record LP features songs from the 1971 film as well as other confectionery-inspired songs, performed by the Golden Orchestra and Chorus.

Sent by Television

Not many modern stories have embedded themselves either as wholly or as firmly in the collective consciousness as *Charlie and the Chocolate Factory* has.

Mel Stuart's film has helped enormously, of course, especially in the US, where its appearance on television amounts these days to a virtual Thanksgiving tradition – paralleling the annual Christmas outing of that other great dual-natured offering, Frank Capra's *It's a Wonderful Life* (1946), whose festive cheer and happy ending belie a similarly dark melancholy underneath.

All this isn't to say the book wouldn't have endured without the film – far from it. After all, as we know, the film only took on its second life when video became popular in the 1980s. Indeed *Charlie* also inspired a video game in 1985. By this decade, *Charlie* had been a bestseller for over twenty years and the rest of Roald Dahl's books habitually stormed the charts, without any help from anyone other than

Inside Charlie's Chocolate Factory

the author and his armies of fans spreading the word from child to child, school to school, country to country, all round the world.

But when a film adaptation of a book is disseminated at least once a year across millions and millions of homes and viewers, and taken almost as much to heart as the book itself is – well, then you might say you've got a Golden Ticket to the infiltration of just about every area of pop culture there is.

It has been endlessly and lovingly parodied everywhere, from *The Simpsons* to *Saturday Night Live* (one of whose skits on *Charlie* shows Glen Wonka, Willy's brother and the factory's accountant, being appalled by the news that he's handed over control of the business to an eight-year-old kid – 'Great . . . I'll tell that to our stockholders when they come down here and beat us bloody with their candy canes'). Innumerable other shows and writers – as well as a surprising number of rappers and other musicians – have referenced or borrowed from it. The whole *Family Guy* episode 'Wasted Talent' (2000) is a tribute to the book/film, as Peter drinks extra Pawtucket Patriot

Andy Samberg as the Jewish Willy Wonka with Ben Stiller in *Saturday Night Live* (2011).

Jeff Richards as Willy Wonka and Amy Poehler as Charlie in the sketch about Glen Wonka (played by ex-vice president Al Gore) in *Saturday Night Live* (2002).

beers to try to win one of the silver scrolls that will get him on a tour of the brewery, whose singing workers are called Chumbawumbas. Instead of hobbling and falling over on his way to greet his guests and surprising them with a somersault and perfect landing

In *Epic Movie* (2007), Crispin Glover parodies 'Willy', a character styled on Johnny Depp's depiction of Willy Wonka in Tim Burton's film.

In *30 Rock* (2013), Jack McBrayer as Kenneth pretends to be a rival network executive, bribing a candidate to steal a script that's in development (referencing the Slugworth sub-plot in the 1971 film).

Inside Charlie's Chocolate Factory

like Wonka, Pawtucket Pat pretends to be gunned down in a drive-by shooting. In the Beer Room, he sings 'Pure Inebriation', and when Peter and Brian sneak off to try out the 'beer that never goes flat' it lifts them off the floor and towards an exhaust fan in the ceiling until they manage to fart their way back down.

Homage to *Willy Wonka* is paid in *South Park* too. In the 'A Ladder to Heaven' episode (2002), Lolly the Candy Man runs a contest for a shopping spree in his store, Lolly's Candy Factory, with the winning ticket acquired by Stan, Kyle, Cartman and Kenny, while the singing cigarette-factory workers in the episode 'Butt Out' (2003) resemble an Oompa-Loompa tribute band.

And the penultimate episode of Tina Fey's *30 Rock* (2013) is built round Kenneth and Jack taking five people (called Charlie, Augustus, Violet, Veruca and Mike), each of them competing to become Jack's successor at NBC, on a tour that is secretly the final part of their interview to decide who should become the network's new president. All the candidates are found wanting and in the end Jack decides that the president should be someone who is pure in heart and loves television.

> *'You like NBC, don't you, Kenneth?'*
> *'I think it's the most wonderful place in the whole wide world.'*
> *'Good. Because I'm giving it to you. The whole thing.'*

The only thing that's missing is a glass elevator to round things off. Tracy probably smashed it to bits during rehearsal.

The Simpsons has a little *Charlie and the Chocolate Factory* obsession. In Season 15's episode 'Simple Simpson' (2004), Homer – whose love of pig meat rivals Charlie Bucket's adoration of cacao-bean derivatives – becomes intrigued by a contest held by (the top-hatted) Farmer Billy's bacon factory, whose Golden Ticket winner will be allowed to visit the hallowed site. Alas, he has to settle for a silver one, and only gets to judge the pig competition at the county fair.

In 'The Ziff Who Came to Dinner' (2004), Artie asks Lisa if her father ever reads stories to her. 'He tried once,' she replies. 'But he got confused and thought the book was real. He's still looking for that chocolate factory. It consumes him.'

Earlier in the series, in 'Lisa's Rival' (1994), there is a Gloop-like German foreign-exchange student, Üter Zörker. He first appears in the 'Treehouse of Horror IV' episode (1993), offering Milhouse a bite of his 'Vengelerstrasse bar. I also have a bag of marzipan Joy Joys . . . mit iodine,' and in 'Treehouse of Horror V' (1994) Üter gets chopped into bratwurst (which you could easily imagine them squeezing through pipes to make). For Diorama-rama day at Springfield Elementary in 'Lisa's Rival', he chooses to do *Charlie and the Chocolate Factory*. Principal Skinner comes to examine Üter's entry but:

> Skinner: *This is just an empty box!*
> Üter [*chocolate smeared round his face and hands*]: *I begged you to look at mine first! I begged you!*

There's also an Ah, Fudge! Factory in downtown Springfield but – as its products are confections of powdered milk, cocoa and caustic chemicals rather than luscious waterfall-mixed chocolate, innovation, imagination and fabulism – its resemblance ends there. It's the setting for one of the educational films shown to Bart's class, this time about the history of chocolate:

> *Welcome to the chocolate factory. I'm Troy McClure . . .*
> *The history of chocolate begins with the ancient Aztecs. In those days, instead of being wrapped in a hygienic package, chocolate was wrapped in a tobacco leaf. And instead of being pure chocolate, like we have today, it was mixed with shredded tobacco. And they didn't eat it – they smoked it!*

Not altogether different from what British children were buying in the eighties, as I say, but there you go. Everyone's comedy is somebody else's tragedy. *Sigh*.

Computer Games Based on the Book and Film

Charlie has proved as fertile an inspiration for creators of video games as it has in every other sphere. A computer game set in the chocolate factory first appeared in 1985 and the idea has been frequently reinvented ever since. Charlie and Willy Wonka have also had their own island within the popular children's online world *Poptropica* since 2012.

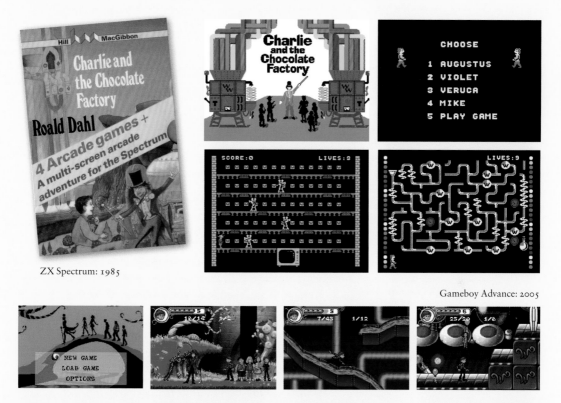

ZX Spectrum: 1985

Gameboy Advance: 2005

Playstation: 2005

Louise Post from the band Veruca Salt, dressed like Veruca Salt at a concert (2006).

Charlie is a popular point of reference for rappers too. 'Monster' on Kanye West's *My Beautiful Dark Twisted Fantasy* album (2010) has the lines 'in that Tonka / colour of Willy Wonka' rapped by Nicki Minaj. Wiz Khalifa in 'Purple Flowers' on his *Yellow Starships* album (2012) says 'Willy Wonka's in my closet, all these flavors / Shop with me you'll get exhausted'. And Boston rapper B-Baz's 'Willy Wonka, Willy Wonka (Interlude)' on his *Genesis* mixtape (2012) refers to his desire to check out Wonka's stock and purchase 'something really special' – undoubtedly meaning the wide variety of delicious chocolate bars with which he likes to keep himself supplied. Ahem.

Other musician fans include the alt-rock band Veruca Salt and, if we expand our remit a little to the chocolate factory's sequel *Charlie and the Great Glass Elevator* (1972), the US indie rock group The Vermicious Knid, who sadly disbanded in 2006. Another great aficionado is Ozzy Osbourne, as Julie Dawn Cole discovered a few years ago when she was introduced to Sharon Osbourne on the set of a music video being produced by Rob Newman. He had grown up next door to the Dahls in the 1960s and his father Robert Newman had been the Quaker Oats Company's representative on the *Willy Wonka* film set, there to keep an eye on the expenses being incurred. As a result, young Rob had also been on set most days and made friends with all the cast – Julie Dawn Cole most firmly and enduringly.

> *Sharon called him over and said, 'You'll never guess who this is!' And he stopped production for half an hour while he peppered me with questions: 'Was the river really chocolate?' and so on! Apparently Kelly Osbourne was desperate to play Veruca Salt in the [Tim Burton] remake but she was too old.*

Inside Charlie's Chocolate Factory

There's also Ozzy's fellow rocker Marilyn Manson, who often recites at the beginning of his concerts the poem Gene Wilder delivers on the SS *Wonkatania* as he and the children travel down the chocolate river ('There's no earthly way of knowing which direction we are going . . .'). He also used it as the prelude to his album *Portrait of an American Family* (1994). The promo single for that album was accompanied by a video showing Manson and his band sailing down a river of blood through a tunnel lined with hideous images. He cites the story as an example of the perils of self-indulgence and self-worship which are – apparently – the true evil. Satan's just a guy with a bad rep – cranky from low blood sugar, perhaps. When it was announced that Burton was making his film, Manson was quoted as saying he was being considered for the role of Wonka, although there seems to be no truth in this. But a source did say that Depp had pictures of Manson and played his music to help hone the darker edge he was giving Wonka, so maybe there's a homage in there somewhere. Or a homage to a homage. Or – let's stop before we eat ourselves.

Australian comedian Matthew Hardy with Julie Dawn Cole.

Australian comic Matthew Hardy was inspired by his love of the film to create a hit two-man comedy show, *Willy Wonka Explained: The Veruca Salt Sessions*. 'I'd been a fan since I first saw it when I was five years old. I was shocked that it ended. I felt like I was one of Charlie Bucket's friends.' But it was Veruca Salt he loved best. 'All that talking back to adults and

A promotional poster for Matthew Hardy's show with Julie Dawn Cole, which first ran in Melbourne (2005).

Inside Charlie's Chocolate Factory

having authority over them – I couldn't believe it!' Whenever he broke up with a girlfriend or moved to a new city or country, he would return to the film, comfort-watching it again and again. He began to wonder why it – and Veruca – had such a hold over him but it wasn't until he was living in the US as an adult that the idea to write a show about his obsession took hold.

He had been invited to give a talk to a teacher friend's class on Long Island about Australia, and during it a pupil started eating his lunch sandwich and said, 'Man, this is scrumdiddlyumptious!' Then on a later visit to a Manhattan bar a woman he was talking to ordered an Everlasting Gobstopper cocktail 'which was written up on the board in the Wonka font,' he says. That's when he mustered the courage to send an email to Julie Dawn Cole's agent asking if he could interview her. She agreed, and out of their talks Hardy constructed a show to take to the Melbourne International Comedy Festival. But then, when Cole agreed to come over from England and help promote it, she said to Hardy, 'Why just promote it? I'm still an actress,' and so it evolved into a two-hander, each playing 'themselves' in therapy, and introducing new elements such as readings from the letters Julie had sent home to her mother while she was filming in Munich.

'As the script took shape we both got really excited about it,' says Hardy. The feeling wasn't misplaced. The show was a smash in Melbourne in 2005 and later at the 2010 Edinburgh Comedy Festival in Scotland.

Hardy still loves Veruca Salt and the film. 'My five-year-old nephew cried the other day at the wedding scene in *Shrek* and he didn't know why. That's the fascinating thing about a well-told story – it's understood, in some way, by everybody.'

Such uses and references are a testament to the widespread nature of *Charlie*'s fame and enduring hold on our hearts and imaginations, depending as they do on an immediate, collective understanding of the original. Their creators know that they can rely on any average audience to get the joke. This is never more true than when it comes to the successful generation of memes: those little snatches of humour, or clutch of film frames, or evocative photos or facial expressions plucked out of their original context, given a little creative twist and packaged

GENE WILDER?

NEVER HEARD OF HIM

INHERITS SUCCESSFUL CHOCOLATE FACTORY

DEVOTES LIFE TO HELPING SICK ANIMALS

Bedridden; makes you wait on him hand and foot

Jumps out of bed the second there's something fun to do

I WANT TOUR DATES!

I WANT TOUR DATES NOW!

up as GIFs or jpegs and sent out into the cyberworld. The infinite adaptability of Wonka's mercurial nature and Gene Wilder's enigmatic portrayal have proved irresistible to the inventors of these little snippets that live or die according to the instantaneous recognition and quick rush of memory and association they induce. They are like catching sight of the spine of a book you love on a friend's shelf – a little reminder of our shared knowledge, a little reminder of a common delight.

There's something about all these jokes, references, spin-offs and memes that chimes happily with the subversive undertow of *Charlie*. Whether Roald Dahl would have seen it like that or whether his feelings about popular 'unauthorized' interpretations and uses of his book would have been the same as those he expressed for the authorized transformation of *Charlie* by Mel Stuart is a matter of conjecture. Does the internet free the anarchist or render him redundant? Discuss animatedly, among yourselves.

Top Chef: Just Desserts

In 2011, America's *Top Chef* programme developed a spin-off series – *Top Chef: Just Desserts* – which concentrated specifically on pastry chefs. To celebrate the fortieth anniversary of the release of *Willy Wonka and the Chocolate Factory*, one of the episodes gathered together the actors who had played the original ticket winners (save Michael Böllner) to be guests and asked the *Top Chef* contestants to create their own edible world of Wonka-ish wonder. The contestants were almost overcome. 'Everyone wants to do this in their life, as a pastry chef,' said the eventual winner, Katzie Guy-Hamilton, who conjured up a carrot patch (slices of cake buried in Oreo soil) and a beehive that dripped real honey. 'And if they don't, they're silly.' Well said, that girl. Except that, trust me, it's not just pastry chefs who long to get the chance.

LEFT: Judge Johnny Iuzzini examines a creation with Paris Themmen, Julie Dawn Cole and fellow judge Hubert Keller.

RIGHT: Contestant Sally Camacho made a wheelbarrow full of Oompa-Loompa crumbles (also called Oompa-Loompa droppings during the show): pistachio financiers, orange dirt and milk-chocolate mousse.

Together they came up with crumbled orange-sugar soil (though its inventor took the odd decision to call it 'Oompa-Loompa droppings', which made it slightly less mouth-watering), green doughnuts, edible wallpaper, peanut butter and jelly macaroons, and a brave, brave attempt at a giant gummy bear. They put together a chocolate fountain, whoopie-pie flowers, gingerbread dragonflies and baked cupcakes in golden eggshells. Altogether, a whipple-scrumptious delight.

In addition to the hundreds of amateur cooks and candymakers whose Roald Dahl-inspired creations can be seen on a thousand blogs, Tumblr, Pinterest and Instagram shrines to their interests, professional chocolatiers, bakers and chefs around the world cite *Charlie* as their childhood inspiration. And, even if they don't, as soon as they reach the headlines they will almost certainly be described as the Willy Wonka of the West Village/pastry/everything from soup to nuts.

Dylan Lauren, daughter of Ralph and creator of the Dylan's Candy Bar chain of stores, remembers seeing the film when she was six, after which she spent years obsessed with sweets and chocolate. She once filled in a college application form that asked candidates to compare themselves to a foodstuff, place or object with an essay on 'Why I Am Like An Everlasting Gobstopper', and after graduating she travelled the

world, discovering new forms of confectionery in far-flung places. She finally realized her chocolate-factory-inspired childhood dream when in 2001 she opened her first Candy Bar in Manhattan. Each store is a miniature Wonka wonderland: the fixtures and fittings are either made out of confectionery (such as the bubblegum-ball-filled stools and candy-mosaic tables) or look like it – mouldings that replicate lashings of dripping chocolate top the shelves, giant glass lollipop trees and huge possibly-chocolate bunnies populate the place.

'Lots of people call me "the Candy Queen" or the modern-day Willy Wonka!' she says in her book *Dylan's Candy Bar: Unwrap Your Sweet Life*. 'But I have yet to figure out how to get a chocolate river running through the middle of America.'

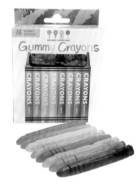

ABOVE:
Dylan's Candy Bar confectionery.

Jacques Torres with
Oompa-Loompas at the
fortieth-anniversary party
of the 1971 film.

Inside Charlie's Chocolate Factory

Wait. Do I smell a sequel or what? Mr Burton, Mr Mendes, when either of you has a minute ...

And what other reference could you possibly reach for when trying to describe master pastry chef and chocolate-maker Jacques Torres? He hosted the fortieth anniversary celebrations for the 1971 film in his New York City chocolate shop and recently designed his new factory in Brooklyn with a cacao-pod-shaped shop, a seventy-foot tunnel, a chocolate-powder room, an ice-cream room, a five-ton chocolate-melter and a layout that allows visitors to watch the assembly line of products as they emerge. As *30 Rock*'s Liz Lemon would say, I would like to go there.

Molecular gastronomist Heston Blumenthal – the man who from his kitchen-slash-laboratory gave the world snail porridge, bacon-and-egg ice cream, sea-jelly eggs and meat fruit, and who probably is the closest thing we have in the UK to a real-life Willy Wonka – once created an entire four-course meal in tribute to his 'childhood hero' from the book he read with 'complete and utter wonderment' when he was a boy. It comprised a lickable wallpaper *amuse-bouche* (apple, sausage and prawn cocktail flavours – not together – made by centrifugally separating the ingredients' components, painting images in the liquids and topping them with the remaining powders to create a flock effect), 'magic mushroom' soup starter (layers of mushroom purée, stock and consommé in red-and-white toadstool caps and set in a woodland scene covered with caramelized puff-pastry leaves and brioches carved and coloured like ceps), Duck à l'Orange for the main course (duck parfait encased in orange and presented to guests in a Terry's Chocolate Orange-style foil wrapper and box), and a chocolate waterfall (made to froth and bubble with liquid nitrogen as it flowed down edible rocks, separating into edible powder and chocolate-flavoured liquid) for dessert. It was served to celebrity guests who rapidly transformed into giggling, delighted children – a reminder of the emotional heft of food and how potent the combination of that and childhood books and memories is and surely will remain.

NK&A®

**WHIPPLE-SCRUMPTIOUS
FUDGEMALLOW DELIGHT**
All About Chocolate

Introduction

The chocolate waterfall, the minty sugar meadows, the boiled-sweet boat, the chewing-gum meal . . . The deliciously vivid images from Roald Dahl's best-loved book have worked like Proust's *madeleines* for millions of readers and viewers around the world for half a century, invoking past rhapsodies and treasured memories. As chocolatier Max Brenner, whose chocolate shops and cafes in the USA, Israel and Australia are visibly inspired by Willy Wonka, says, 'Most people think of chocolate like *Charlie and the Chocolate Factory*, as fun and happiness, childhood memories and romance.'

The story of *Charlie* is inextricably linked in people's minds with the fabulous confections it describes and our enduring passion for their real-life approximations. There has been a stream (if not an actual chocolate river) of confectionery products that seek to exploit this link during the forty-odd years since the release of the 1971 film.

Whipple-Scrumptious Fudgemallow Delight

161

A 1972 trade brochure for salesmen, showcasing Willy Wonka's Candies. This new brand was owned by Quaker Oats, and it launched with two products: Super Skrunch and Peanut Butter Oompas. Quaker Oats promoted them through their popular Quisp and Cap'n Crunch cereals, including a Golden Ticket coupon in 10 million packs of Cap'n Crunch (for seven cents towards the purchase of Willy Wonka's Candies). The company also produced a mail-order Willy Wonka's Candy Factory kit (see page 140 for an example).

As we've already heard, the original Willy Wonka's Peanut Butter Oompa-Loompa Cups that Quaker Oats intended to launch and promote with the help of the Mel Stuart/Gene Wilder film never quite made it to market. (Though the simpler M&M-style Oompas did quite well till the early 1980s.) However, by the time Tim Burton's film came out in 2005, things were better organized.

In the years between the two films, Quaker Oats (who owned the rights to the Wonka name, which Roald had signed over as part of the film funding agreement) had been bought and sold on by various companies. In 1976, one of them launched Wonka Bars, which were graham crackers (light digestive biscuits) dipped in milk chocolate. (Sorry if you're salivating, British readers – they never made it over to your side of the pond. Sorry too, actually, to any salivating American readers – they were discontinued in 2010. However many of you are dribbling, it was clearly not enough.)

The Wonka brand came to rest with its current owner Nestlé in 1988. Out of their testing vats, tubes, flasks, bubbling beakers and whirring mixers came the Wonka Xploder bar (milk chocolate mixed with popping candy) and Wonka biscuits. Then – after Nestlé decided to (cover your ears, purists) expand the brand into confectionery products as well as chocolate – came Everlasting Gobstoppers (they're not, incidentally; magical manufacturers may work like that, but modern Western capitalism does not) and Wonka Nerds in just about every flavour under the sun, including snozzberry. They also produced Wonkalate (a purple chocolate bar studded with the aforementioned snozzberry Nerds) and Oompas (peanut-butter, chocolate and strawberry flavoured originally, then chewy fruity varieties including, in the UK, mashed potato, caterpillar and snozzberry again).

To celebrate the release of Tim Burton's film in 2005, in the UK Nestlé produced some of the chocolate that appeared in the film and that more closely resembled the bars mentioned in the book: the Whipple-Scrumptious Fudgemallow Delight Bar, the Nutty Crunch Surprise and the Triple Dazzle Caramel. They had a short but lucrative and – if I may insert personal testimony here – absolutely delicious run.

Bringing the story up to date, Nestlé launched its Wonka Exceptionals

One of the Wonka
Inventing Room range
produced for the Wonka
boutique at Sweet! in
Hollywood, Los Angeles.

range in the US, comprising the Wonka Scrumdiddlyumptious Chocolate
Bar (named after one in the 1971 film), as well as the Wonka Chocolate
Waterfall Bar (white and milk chocolate swirled together, though not by
waterfall – doubtless for modern health and safety reasons that Wonka
did not have to contend with). The third of these, the Wonka Domed
Dark Chocolate Bar, contained dark chocolate topped with milk-
chocolate buttons. (But not Cadbury's Chocolate Buttons. That would
be very confusing.) When the new line first hit the shelves in America
there were ten Golden Tickets to be found in Wonka Exceptionals bars
and bags, each one granting the finder a trip round the world. (It was
not, alas, tradeable for a lifetime's supply of chocolate.)

Later, the Wonka Triple Dazzle Caramel was resurrected (this time as a
sea-salted caramel-filled bar instead of caramel covered in white
chocolate as the original bar had been) and a chocolate-covered fudge
bar called Wonka Fantabulous Fudge was introduced. They were
discontinued in 2012, but the UK at least was able to fill the void a year
later with the invention of a new range of Wonka Bars – Millionaire's
Shortbread (biscuit pieces in a caramel-paste filling covered in
chocolate), Crème Brûlée (filled with vanilla cream and crunchy caramel
bits) and Chocolate Nice Cream (vanilla filling topped with chocolate
sauce – to mimic a bowl of ice cream covered in chocolate, you
understand).

Nestlé continues to reimagine their Wonka brand. They launched
Wonka chocolate in Australia in 2013 and now also have the licence to

create ice cream under the Wonka brand. We can only hope that we'll soon be able to buy hot ice cream for cold days.

Willy Wonka remains an irresistible inspiration to chocolate-makers and retailers everywhere. Recently Sweet!, a confectionery store in Hollywood, created a boutique that features some of the favourite moments and creations from the book (even the square sweets that look round are there). And, of course, they've included some of the other 'more than 200 new kinds of chocolate bars, each with a different centre, each far sweeter and creamier and more delicious than anything the other chocolate factories can make!' that Grandpa Joe so excitedly tells Charlie about to keep their minds off their empty stomachs every evening. Scenes in the windows show possible solutions to questions children commonly ask about the book ('How does Wonka transport his luscious products?') and give further ideas of what amazing sights the factory might still hold for its new owner, such as a volcano for toasting marshmallows.

A selection of old and new Wonka confectionery.

For the Love of Chocolate

Why do we love chocolate so? Partly it's simply because of its and our chemical and biological make-up. Millions of years of evolution taught us that sweet nuts and berries are rarely poisonous and that the ingestion of sugar whenever possible is a good rule to live by, especially when your lifestyle roaming the tundra or savannah required fast and frequent bursts of energy to escape predatory mammoths (or, unless the iconic films of the late sixties lie, damn dirty talking apes bent on man's destruction/exploitation for laryngeal experimentation).

But this cannot be the whole explanation, otherwise we would prize most highly pure sugar, or the purest form in which we could get it, which would put sweets and candy in a position unassailable by chocolate, diluted as it is by interlopers like fats, milk and, y'know, cocoa.

And cocoa is the key. It is one of the most complicated flavoursome substances around, containing over twelve hundred chemical components that interact in a practically uncomputable number of ways to deliver a taste much more interesting and rewarding than the thin, monotonous taste of sugar (whatever fruit or other flavours you add to make it into sweets). Plus cocoa contains a healthy handful of psychoactive compounds like caffeine, theobromine (the ones that help keep you awake and alert and make you wonder why Augustus Gloop wasn't a little more aware of the imminent danger of being sucked up the pipe), phenylalanine and phenylethylamine (connected with the production of feelings of happiness) and anandamide (which is very like the chemical in cannabis that causes smokers to get high).

But we must pay due respect to the sugar, and the fat and the milk it's mixed with. They add a creamy richness, a smooth melting consistency – maybe with an extra layer (literally) of interest thrown in via a wafer, or caramel or a nutty filling – and a

Augustus Gloop in the chocolate river, illustrated by Quentin Blake.

Inside Charlie's Chocolate Factory

super-sweet taste of which it seems that, as a species, as individuals, we will simply never tire. Sales of chocolate don't suffer in a recession. It delivers too much pleasure for the number of pennies it costs for it to fall off any but the most stringent shopping lists.

Some nations – imagine! – are only just beginning to taste the joys in store. At the moment, the growing middle classes in countries like Russia, China, India and Brazil are responsible for over half the annual sales growth in the retail confectionery market. As soon as – or as long as – we have any spare income, it seems, we want chocolate. From the dimmest reaches of the past to the very modernest of modern times, it still holds us in its thrall.

For most of us, however, the greatest pull of chocolate – as with most foods but especially the sweet treats of childhood – is emotional. In this of course it is much like the books we read when young. Most of us remember our first taste of chocolate – maybe sharing someone's stash, or given to us by a fond grandparent or weary parent, or maybe bought with pocket money when finances and palate were ready to graduate from penny chews and liquorice bootlaces. It's a rite of passage and, just as we do with the books we consume as children, we remain passionately attached to the products we first come to know. Manufacturers change the formulations and recipes at their peril. Those who lived through the traumatic replacement of brown Smarties with blue in 1988 (blue – whoever heard of a blue Smartie!), or the substitution of the foil wrapping of the KitKat with a plastic abomination, or the disappearance of the Caramello know whereof I speak. Time does not heal. Such moments and memories unite generations.

We tend to grow out of a love of simple sweets like penny chews and into a love of chocolate. Apart from its innate, sugary, food-of-the-gods attractions, our love stays fresh because however old you get, chocolate retains the lure of the forbidden. When you're young, you're not allowed to eat as much as you want because of wearisome adult concerns about tooth decay and appetites ruined for proper meals (parents being inexplicably immune to the advertisers' assurances that a Finger of Fudge is both Full of Cadbury Goodness and enough to Give Your Kids a Treat Until It's Time to Eat, or that a Milky Way is The

In the Sweet!
Hollywood store,
Los Angeles.

Inside Charlie's Chocolate Factory

Sweet You Can Eat Between Meals Without Ruining Your Appetite), and because the aforementioned pocket money will only go so far. When you are older, you find – if you are lucky – that your endless appetite for it lessens, or (if you are unluckily normal) that the desire not to out-Gloop Augustus in your gluttony or appearance will keep you from indulging nearly as fully as you would like. Life is just great like that.

Still, though, opening a bar of chocolate that we have loved since childhood carries the same nostalgic pleasures and comfort as opening a favourite book. Re-immersing ourselves in a fictional world filled with wonders, we roll these round our minds like chocolate in our mouths, slowly letting the delicious notions, the delicate flavours of someone else's imagination, flood out and delight our senses. Putting the two together has a sweetness all of its own.

A sample of what you can purchase from Sweet!

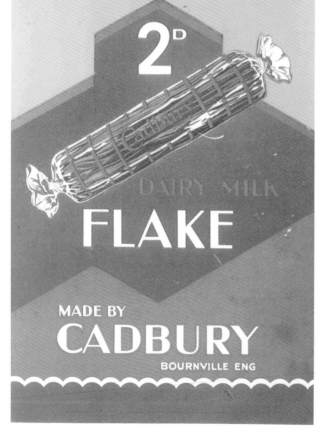

Flake packaging: 1922 (top); 1935 (bottom).

All About Chocolate

There are two ways you can go with chocolate. You can take the gourmet route and become a cacao-bean epicure (or 'someone who is dainty with his eating' for those who don't remember their *Matilda*), never letting anything under eighty-per-cent cocoa solids past your lips and learning to distinguish between estates and harvests, appreciating the textures and aromas as the chocolate transforms from solid to liquid on your tongue, and revelling in its bittersweet complexities.

Or you can go the other route. You know – the tasty route. The fun route. The delicious, sugary, creamy route whose pleasure stations are marked 'Dairy Milk', 'KitKat', 'Creme Egg', 'Milky Way' and on and on into the sweetly shimmering distance.

In many ways, you would expect Roald Dahl, a man who adored good food and who became a self-taught expert on wine, to have gone down the first road. But in fact he loved what most of us love – the ordinary stuff, the bars available by the handful at every supermarket, newsagent, train station, airport, kiosk, drugstore, bodega and most points in between.

Inside Charlie's Chocolate Factory

Not, of course, that they were so commonly available – or in some cases, available at all – when Roald was growing up in England in the 1920s. The Cadbury's Dairy Milk bar existed and had done since 1905, the result of feverish experimentation by the company in a quest to invent an extra-creamy product that would rival the Swiss milk chocolate that was coming to dominate the market. And the same was true of such creations as the Flake, Fry's Turkish Delight (a rose-flavoured filling covered in milk chocolate) and Rowntrees' Walnut Whip (a marshmallow-stuffed chocolate case topped with the nut – no word on whether squirrels were used), but chocolate was primarily the domain of adults.

'We small boys and girls were much more inclined to spend our money on either sweets or toffees or on some of the many very cheap and fairly disgusting things that lay about in open cardboard boxes all over the sweet shop,' Roald recalls in *Memories with Food at Gipsy House*, the last book he wrote (with his wife Liccy), which was published a year after he died. 'Sherbet-suckers and gobstoppers and liquorice bootlaces and aniseed

Original Bournville chocolate packaging, 1908.

The Dairy Milk wrapper, originally lilac and red, was purple from 1920.

Fruit and Nut wrapper, 1970s.

Roald Dahl with his prep-school tuck box in 1924, from *Boy*, illustrated by Quentin Blake (Puffin, 2008).

balls and all the rest of them, and we did not mind that the liquorice was made from rat's blood and the sherbet from sawdust.'

In 1929, Roald was thirteen and went away to Repton, the famous Derbyshire boarding school. Here, his confectionery horizons were expanded. One of the most famous – and most joyful – passages in *Boy* tells the story of how every pupil in his House would occasionally receive a plain grey cardboard box, 'and this, believe it or not, was a present from the great chocolate manufacturers, Cadbury'. Inside were twelve chocolate bars – eleven new inventions and one 'control' bar – for them to test, mark out of ten and comment on via a form that was enclosed in the box. 'Too subtle for the common palate,' is one comment he remembered writing down.

As well as the delight of the chocolate itself, those gifts from Cadbury made Roald realize that chocolate didn't just come to exist – it had to be invented. That in every chocolate factory there were whole departments, whole laboratories devoted to confecting new, exciting bars and sweets. He recalled in *Boy*:

> *I used to picture a long white room . . . with pots of chocolate and fudge and all sorts of other delicious fillings bubbling away on the stoves, while men and women in white coats moved between the bubbling pots, tasting and mixing and concocting their wonderful new inventions. I used to imagine working in one of these labs and suddenly I would come up with something so absolutely unbearably delicious that I would grab it in my hand and go rushing . . . right into the office of the great Mr Cadbury himself . . . [He] would take a small bite. He would roll it round his mouth. Then all at once, he would leap up from his chair, crying, 'You've got it! You've done it! It's a miracle!' He would slap me on the back and shout, 'We'll sell it by the million! We'll sweep the world with this one! How on earth did you do it? Your salary is doubled!'*

It hardly needs saying that these daydreams, and Roald's enduring love of chocolate (during his years working for Shell in London he began

Inside Charlie's Chocolate Factory

saving the silver wrappers from his daily bars, moulding them into the beginnings of a ball to which he added and kept on his desk in his writing hut until he died) formed the background inspiration and material for *Charlie and the Chocolate Factory*. The real thing sounds almost as good as the fantasy.

As if being Cadbury guinea pigs were not great fortune enough, Roald and his fellow students were also of prime chocolate-purchasing and consuming age during the most extraordinary few years in the history of modern chocolate.

Roald's ball of foil chocolate-bar wrappers.

The Golden Age of Chocolate

The fruit of the *Theobroma* ('food of the gods') *cacao* had already come a long way from its earliest use as a cold, bitter drink beloved of the Mayans and the Aztecs for its supposedly divine associations and miraculous strengthening, aphrodisiacal qualities. In 1528, Hernán Cortés had presented the Spanish king Charles V with a gift of cacao beans and offered the quite helpful suggestion that someone should try adding sugar to the confections made from these. He established a plantation of them in the name of Spain while out in Mexico toppling Montezuma and the rest of the Aztec empire who, alas, found that those strengthening properties of *xocolatl*, as they called it, were no defence against a set of conquistadors running rampant through the indigenous populations of Mesoamerica.

From there, its fame and popularity spread rapidly across Europe – first, among the nobles and aristocrats who could afford and were thought worthy of this special drink, then, as changing import taxes and cheaper methods of production and transportation came in, on through the masses. Chocolate made its first appearance in the US in 1765, when Irish chocolate-maker John Hanan imported some cacao beans from the West Indies to Dorchester, Massachusetts. He and a doctor, James Baker (chocolate was

Botanical drawings of the cacao bean that used to hang on the wall of Roald's home, Gipsy House.

JOHN CADBURY AND HIS FAMILY.
Standing, at back : John ; Richard.
Sitting : Maria ; Mrs. John Cadbury (Candia Barrow) ; (on her lap) Henry ; Edward
John Cadbury ; George.

ABOVE LEFT:
George Cadbury (1888).

ABOVE RIGHT:
John Cadbury and his
family (1840s).

at the time thought to have medicinal properties), built the first American chocolate factory. In 1893, an entrepreneur called Milton Snavely Hershey became mesmerized by a miniature chocolate factory displayed at the World's Fair in Chicago, bought it, took it home and started experimenting. Before long, he decided to sell his successful caramel company, which he'd set up in 1887, in order to start a new venture. His decision ('I'll stake everything on chocolate!') became famous and the success of the Hershey company was unprecedented.

Meanwhile, in Great Britain the chocolate industry was dominated by three firms – Cadbury, Rowntrees and Fry. They were all owned by Quaker families, whose religious beliefs in the evils of alcohol made businesses based on alternative beverages very appealing (cocoa then being used mainly as a drink). By the turn of the century, Fry's had merged with Cadbury, and Rowntrees had expanded into new premises covering twenty-four acres. Once they and Europe had recovered from the First World War and the Depression thereafter, the chocolate-makers were ready to embrace mass manufacturing, and the spirit of innovation that would give Roald Dahl most of his favourite bars swept through the industry.

Inside Charlie's Chocolate Factory

Between 1930 and 1937, these British companies produced most of what have since become enduring classics and constant bestsellers: the Crunchie, 'the lovely Aero' (as Roald reverently refers to it in *Memories of Food*), Roses, Quality Street, Black Magic, KitKats (originally known as the Chocolate Crisp and inspired by an employee's note in the Rowntrees suggestion box, requesting a snack that a man could take with his lunch to work), Rolos and Smarties (and – for older readers – Caramello, which alas has since gone to the great roaster in the sky).

On the other side of the Atlantic, other classics were also being developed. In 1930 at the Mars headquarters in Minneapolis, Minnesota, Frank Mars and his son Forrest came up with a peanut variation on the nougat, caramel and chocolate bar they'd invented in 1924 – the Milky Way – and the new version was called Snickers, after the family horse. (There seems to be some strange affinity between candy names and horses. George Smith, owner of the Bradley-Smith candy company and inventor of the lollipop, named his creation after his favourite racehorse, Lolly Pop.) The Mars family then followed that up in 1932 with the 3 Musketeers bar, which was essentially three pieces of different-flavoured whipped chocolate covered in more chocolate.

ABOVE LEFT: Joseph Rowntree (with grandchild on knee), who joined his brother, Henry Isaac Rowntree, founder of the firm, in the business in 1869.

ABOVE MIDDLE: (TOP) Easter eggs being hand-decorated on the Rowntrees production line in 1930; (BOTTOM) workers packing fruit pastilles at the Rowntrees factory in York in 1910.

ABOVE RIGHT: The founder, Henry Isaac Rowntree.

(Dear British readers: the Snickers bar was called Marathon in the UK until 1990, when Mars decided to standardize the brand and presumably felt that Brits were mature enough now to handle the fact that 'Snickers' sounded a lot like 'knickers' which is British-English for 'panties'. Also, what the British and Europeans know as the Milky Way is a product very like the American 3 Musketeers bar, and the European Mars bar is what the Americans know as a Milky Way. US readers: strike all that, and reverse it. Sort of.)

In 1933, Frank told Forrest that America wasn't big enough for both of them and that he had to leave and start a business in some other country. Forrest (whose factory Roald would gleefully tour many years later) took himself and the foreign rights for the (American) Milky Way to Britain, where he developed a new, chunkier version of his bestselling product and called it the Mars bar. The British were so grateful, they bought two million of them in the first year and have done nothing but improve on that figure ever since. Incidentally, Forrest also devised the now-famous Maltesers, which were first called Energy Balls until he noticed that, as Roald Dahl put it, 'this made the public smile' and changed the name.

Roald remained a fan of these bars all his life. No matter how elegant a meal had just been served at Gipsy House, afterwards with coffee he would bring out the selection of KitKats, Mars bars, Flakes and so on that he kept in a red plastic box. He wrote in *Memories with Food*:

Roald's box of chocolate treats, which was passed around after dinner at Gipsy House.

The dates [about chocolate] are milestones in history and should be seared into the memory of every child in the country . . . In music the equivalent would be the golden age when compositions by Bach and Mozart and Beethoven were given to us. In painting it was the equivalent of the Renaissance in art and the advent of the Impressionists towards the end of the nineteenth century. In literature it was Tolstoy and Balzac and Dickens. I tell you, there has been nothing else like it . . . and there never will be.

Inside Charlie's Chocolate Factory

Advertisement for
a Mars chocolate
bar – later to be
known as the
Mars Bar, 1947.

Whipple-Scrumptious Fudgemallow Delight

AFTER EIGHT

WAFER THIN
CHOCOLATE
MINTS

Crisp to Crunch-More to Munch-

Everyone Loves

Maltesers

FULL-CREAM MILK
CHOCOLATE
COATING!

MUNCHY MALT
HONEYCOMB
CENTRES!

Yes! Maltesers are mouth-
watering—*and* magnificent
value too! No wonder over
seven millions of them are
bought every day. Plenty
for everyone in the big box
—and it still costs only 1/6d.

ANOTHER SWEET TREAT BY MARS

TOP LEFT: An early advert for
After Eights. In the 1960s,
Rowntrees chocolatier Brian
Sollit was asked to create a
luxurious chocolate with a
peppermint fondant centre. And
thus After Eights were born.

TOP RIGHT: Another Rowntrees
favourite was KitKat, which
launched in the 1930s.

BOTTOM LEFT: Magazine
advert for Maltesers made
by Mars (*c.* 1954).

BOTTOM RIGHT: A 1935
display heralding the launch
of Aero bars by Rowntrees.
The aerated chocolate
was the first of its kind and
it enabled Rowntrees to
successfully compete with
rival company Cadbury's.

SQUARE SWEETS THAT
LOOK ROUND
What the Critics and Fans Say

Inside Charlie's Chocolate Factory

Introduction

In 1988, Roald Dahl was asked to be on the Kingman Committee, which had been set up to help devise the English element of the new national curriculum in Britain. He agreed, but quickly – and publicly – fell out with the rest of the board on the subject of whether Enid Blyton should be embraced by schools. Roald said yes because children loved her and she got them reading. (Not that he himself was a fan of her books, or indeed of the woman herself. Having spent an evening playing bridge with her once years before, he found her to have 'the mind of a child'.) The rest of the committee disagreed and Roald resigned his place.

Roald Dahl always insisted that his primary goal in writing for children was to entertain them. Without that, after all, nothing else could follow – no joy in reading, no notion of books as a source of fun or pleasure, let alone any chance to educate or edify. In an interview from the journal *Children's Literature in Education* in 1990, the year he died, Roald Dahl said:

> *A good children's book teaches the uses of words, the joy of playing with language. Above all, it helps children learn not to be frightened of books. Once they get through a book and enjoy it, they realize that books are something they can cope with. If my books can help children become readers, then I feel I have accomplished something important.*

PREVIOUS SPREAD:
A young fan's drawing of a scene from *Charlie and the Chocolate Factory.*

OPPOSITE:
Roald Dahl in his writing hut at Gipsy House (*c.* 1985).

Of course, an author's stated intention or message doesn't necessarily stop other people interpreting – or misinterpreting – a work in their own way, through the prism of their own understanding, priorities and (arguably) prejudices. And when the work is as spikily idiosyncratic, provoking and altogether mould-breaking a book as *Charlie and the Chocolate Factory*, and it bursts on to a scene as calm, gentle and protective of its readers as children's book publishing was in 1964 – well, expecting the critics to stay away from that was like expecting wasps to stay away from honey, cows from clover or Augustus Gloop from a chocolate river. In this chapter, we look at some of the things that have been seen in *Charlie* by various interested and appalled parties – and also at how he has nevertheless somehow managed to delight readers in their millions over the years.

Augustus Gloop in the river, in the 2005 film.

Inside Charlie's Chocolate Factory

A Book Like Candy

The rumblings of dissatisfaction among librarians, some parents and a number of academic critics about the crudity and corrupting nature of Roald's writing (present ever since the publication of *James and the Giant Peach* and Ethel L. Heins's objections to his 'violent exaggerations of language' and gross characterizations) gathered force after the announcement that *Charlie* was to be made into a film. This spilled over into the public domain in 1972 when Roald sent a chapter (about Marvin Prune) that had been cut from *Charlie* to the *Horn Book Magazine*, thinking that the highly regarded American journal that specialized in children's literature might be interested in publishing it. Instead, the editor printed a piece by Canadian children's writer Eleanor Cameron, which included in its attack on her fellow Canadian Marshall McLuhan (media theorist and champion of television as part of the modern collective consciousness) an almost more virulent assault on *Charlie* and, it seemed to many (including Roald), on Roald Dahl himself. Cameron called the novel 'one of the most tasteless books ever written for children'.

The book was like candy, she said: 'Delectable and soothing while we are undergoing the brief sensory pleasure it affords but leaves us poorly nourished with our taste dulled for better fare.' What *The Times* saw as a 'funny' book shot through with 'zany pathos', Cameron condemned as a 'phony presentation of poverty and its phony humour, which is based on punishment with overtones of sadism'. She objected to the 'hypocrisy' of the author's claim that books are better than television when *Charlie* itself 'is like nothing so much as one of the more specious television shows'. She wondered if its tone, 'the using

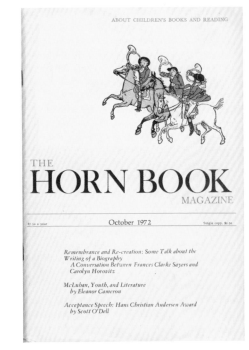

The *Horn Book Magazine*, featuring Eleanor Cameron's initial article in October 1972.

of the Oompa-Loompas' and the final indifference to the wishes of the grandparents harmed young readers.

> *Many adults see all this as humorous and delightful, and I am aware that most children, when they're young, aren't particularly aware of sadism as such, or see it differently from the way an adult sees it and so call* Charlie *'a funny book'.*

It is, she averred, 'a book that diminishes the human spirit, that emphasizes all those *Clockwork Orange* qualities which are destroying the society children are growing up in: callousness, lack of any emotion but the hyped-up one of getting kicks out of the pain and misfortune of others and depicting all this as funny, and delightful etc.'

Roald replied angrily to her essay, finding her positing of harm being done to children by *Charlie* 'the ultimate effrontery', in view of the fact that earlier in the essay, she seems to link a writer's moral character with the 'goodness' – or otherwise – perceived in his books by asserting that 'his worth as a human being . . . is always mercilessly revealed in his writing'. Roald said he'd written it for his beloved, injured son Theo and his other children, for whom he estimates he has made up five thousand bedtime stories over the years. The idea that he would write something that would do them harm 'is too ghastly to contemplate . . . an insensitive and a monstrous implication'.

Cameron replied, denying this charge and reiterating her basic objections, and there that particular matter was left to rest, but of course the underlying criticism and dislike among those of the same mindset as Cameron did not go away. Even *Charlie*'s editor at Knopf, Virginie Fowler, had written a letter to Roald Dahl asking him to tone down the vulgarity ('the whole image of smelling, stinking garbage makes for a crude image . . . one is a bit revolted and unnecessarily too'), and arguing that he shouldn't keep commenting on an adult level but stay 'on the child's side where the book should be'.

To such critics, *Charlie and the Chocolate Factory* is vulgar and panders to children's basest instincts (for immediate gratification, for violence, for mockery and derision of those less fortunate) and indulging

their worst appetites for everything from sweets to vengeance. It does
not do what children's books should do: teach a moral lesson, deepen
understanding, cultivate compassion and educate readers in the ways of
empathy – in all, be a civilizing, not anarchic, force in their lives.

This conception of children's literature as a weapon of morality is an
old one. The very first books intended specifically for children – a
market that emerged in the eighteenth century – were all heavily
didactic things and more offensive to our modern sensibilities than
Roald Dahl's writing has ever been. Those early books tended to be very
concerned with children learning to be good boys and girls (for
example, in *The History of Little Goody Two-Shoes*, published in 1765,
whose heroine's name still lives on as shorthand for smug virtuousness)
and especially to be good Christians. The full title of James Janeway's
1795 bestseller, *A Token for Children: Being an Exact Account of the
Conversion, Holy and Exemplary Lives and Joyful Deaths of Several
Young Children*, gives a sense of what was thought both necessary and

Cover of the 1888 American edition of *Goody Two-Shoes*, published by McLoughlin Bros, New York.

first, and you could barely turn a page of any Victorian author's *oeuvre* without a golden-haired child expiring while extolling the virtues of the Lord who was about to gather it to His bosom at what less saintly folk might feel to be an unfairly young age.

It is a conception of children's literature that has not died as readily as yesteryear's pious orphans did and it may not ever do so entirely. Bringing up children is hard. 'Children are only half-civilized,' as Roald once put it to Polly Toynbee in a 1985 *Guardian* interview. 'They are tougher, coarser and they laugh at things that make us squirm.' So parents, teachers and society at large will cling on to anything that helps them in their endeavours.

You might argue that there is no 'should' in literature – that people, including children, are free to read and write whatever they like, for entertainment, edification and for anything else in-between. A more practical and possibly more effective argument (if it's the aforementioned exhausted parents you're trying to convince) might be that you've got to catch the little monsters first before you can start drilling

appropriate at the time. A few decades later, dominating the readership was Mary Martha Sherwood's *The History of the Fairchild Family* in which Emily, Lucy and Henry Fairchild are taught to recognize their 'human depravity' and work towards their salvation over the course of three lengthy volumes. Two neighbouring children die in the

Inside Charlie's Chocolate Factory

manners, politeness and finer feelings into them, and suggesting that lassoing them with a good story might be an effective means of doing so.

More compelling – I think – is the view many of Roald's supporters have put forward over the years, which is that *Charlie and the Chocolate Factory* has, underneath all the fantastical bells, whistles, gobstoppers and multicoloured fruit drops, a wholly traditional moral at its heart – which is simply: be good, and be rewarded. Or, in moral terms: being like Charlie – thoughtful, kind, unselfish, not greedy – is a good thing, deserving of recognition and acclaim. Being selfish, spoiled, gluttonous – um, not so much.

'Hurrah!' you may say. 'That's told the critics. Can we all go back to reading for fun now?'

No. Because this, runs the counterargument, makes Roald Dahl a hypocrite. By appealing to children's worst natures as they read but punishing them for very traditional transgressions (rudeness, greed, embracing terrible habits) within the story, so the argument goes, he is attempting to have his subversive, maverick, child-pleasing cake and eat it too – for he still gets to push a conservative, 'adult' agenda underneath.

There is, you might legitimately sigh at this point, no pleasing some people.

But for those wedded to the idea of Roald as a cake-eating hypocrite, we might first take a moment to think back to what it was like to be – and to read as – a child. 'Get down on your knees for a week,' he once said, 'to remember what it's like when the people with power literally loom over you.'

Adults may call a great greedy-guts being sucked up a pipe or bumptious horrors having their swollen bodies (and metaphorically swollen heads) thoroughly squished pandering to base instincts. Children call it natural justice, too often unpractised in the real world. This is because children are unblinking reactionaries. Far from experiencing Roald Dahl as a hypocrite who smuggles a conservative message in underneath a child-pleasing exterior, I suspect they admire his consistency – as might some of his affrighted adult readers if they looked a bit longer at the book rather than running off screaming in the opposite direction. Children enjoy a bit of authoritarianism when it

Roald Dahl in the RAF
during the Second
World War, illustrated
by Quentin Blake on
the cover of *Going
Solo* (Puffin, 2001).

comes from someone who understands. Roald knew only too well that it can be both rightly and wrongly used, from his school experiences, his time with the RAF during the war and his dealings with doctors. Nothing makes children feel more secure – and therefore freer in every psychologically important way – than boundaries. They know, as the smallest, weakest members of the human tribe, at some deep, self-preserving level that chaos is only something to be enjoyed if it is temporary and can eventually be brought under control, and that is ultimately what Roald Dahl's stories provide. Survival depends on stability. Roald's long-time illustrator Quentin Blake remembers the first time he saw the author give one of his annual Christmas readings to an audience full of children at the National Theatre in London.

> *He seemed to speak individually to everyone . . . as he did in all his books. He immediately made you feel all right, as though being visited by a seasoned, reliable family doctor. It was this tone of voice – about to let you into some useful secrets of the ways of the world – that gives his stories at least part of their hypnotic fascination for the young.*

And if that family doctor is as likely to prescribe you Smarties to cheer you up, saying they're pills to make you better, what child would ever complain?

What are we to make of the recurring complaint that there is a sadistic element to Roald Dahl's writing for children? This is most evident in *Charlie* in the pleasure Roald seems to take, and therefore encourages his readers to take, in the humiliating punishments devised for most of the ticket holders. And what of the complaints about his misanthropy? And the 'fact' that although Roald writes for children, and children love his books to bits (often literally – my own copy of *Charlie* is a mass of disarrayed dog-eared pages just about kept between its Faith Jaques covers with browning Sellotape), he does not actually seem to like them any more, really, than he does adults?

Inside Charlie's Chocolate Factory

This too, perhaps, betrays a lack of memory of childhood. We knew when we were young that we were vile: the evidence was all around us in the endless petty squabbles, the fights, the rigorously and frequently cruelly maintained pecking order, the constant competition for resources – our primitive brains translating the ancient struggles for survival on the savannah into scrabbling for the best toy, bits of sports kit or spot in the playground. God, we were *horrible*.

In *Charlie*, lying underneath the glorious page-turning entertainments laid on by the factory tour are deeper pleasures – like the recognition that children can be unpleasant and unrewarding company and frequently deserve a good squash in a Juicing Room. However much parents and teachers insisted otherwise, we knew it to be the truth then, and children still know it to be the truth today. I will always remember the relief when I first read *Charlie and the Chocolate Factory* and realized that I was in the company of a truthful adult, who was prepared to admit that what most of his ilk asked of us and of each other – to always be good, polite and respectful – was an impossible ideal. I don't think it had too deleterious an effect on my moral standards either. I understood that you needed to have an ideal but I had learned that it was an ideal and not a realistic goal constantly missed.

Roald liked children enough to let them in on adult truths. He liked them enough to devote months and years of his life to creating whizzing, popping, delirium-inducing fantasies for them – all the rush of sugar, none of the cavities! You'd think people would be more grateful.

Incidentally, I think the fact that it is always the extreme punishments meted out to Augustus *et al.* that are cited by the sadism-pushers is just another example of how distant adult critics are from child readers. All of the latter know that the true pain caused in the book is by the number of attempts it takes Charlie to find his Golden Ticket. Once – fine. Expected that. Two – OK. Just means he'll definitely get one next ti– . . . Wait, three? He doesn't get it in the first bar he buys with the gutter money? You've got to be kidding me! The reader writhes in the exquisite agony of anticipation for what seems at that age like days. But that's not sadism. That's good storytelling.

Amid all this complaining, let us not lose sight of the fact that there have always been people who 'get' Roald in general and who 'got' *Charlie* from the moment it emerged from its long gestation, blinking, into the light.

They have tended to be the people who, like the early reviewer in *The New York Times*, recognized straight away that although it seemed like a break with every convention and tradition of writing for children (and indeed was, of many of them), it was fundamentally a modern version of that most ancient of forms – the fairy tale.

Charlie Bucket moves from rags to riches, rewarded for his virtue like Cinderella, with his peers punished as swiftly as her ugly sisters, and children appreciate that these things are not to be taken literally. They know that a Golden Ticket, a lifetime's supply of chocolate and the gift of a factory full of Oompa-Loompas are not likely to feature prominently in their futures but that they stand for the resolution of any besetting difficulty, from intractable maths homework to divorcing parents. They constitute a promise that this too shall pass. They know that Charlie's poverty and starvation are not realism but melodrama and that his endurance of them is a symbol of and inspiration for anyone starved of opportunity or expression, or who is ostracized from a group (an experience granted most children at one point or another), like Charlie is from the rest of the chocolate-scoffing world.

Once you look at it this way, a lot of criticism becomes redundant. The 'vulgarity' is the modern version of the broad, bright strokes with which the classic fairy tales, their heroes, villains, treasures and quests were painted. The sadism becomes part of the tradition of extremes required by the form. 'In writing for children,' as Roald put it, 'you have to exaggerate a million times in order to ram the point home.' Symbolism, not realism, is the order of the day. Charlie is an Everychild, with whom the reader can identify. If that makes us 'boring little buggers' by association, so be it. Who cares at that age if the devil gets all the best tunes, as long as the angel gets all the best sweets?

And, as with most fairy tales, the effect is cautionary. In *The Uses of Enchantment: The Meaning and Importance of Fairy Tales*, Bruno

Bettelheim suggests that fairy tales are a way of allowing children to learn at arm's length about violence and brutality, and about human nature:

> . . . *the source of much that goes wrong in life is due to our very own natures – the propensity of all men for acting aggressively, asocially, selfishly, out of anger and anxiety. Instead we want our children to believe that inherently all men are good. But children know that they are not always good; and often, even when they are, they would prefer not to be.*

The Brothers Grimm, Hans Christian Andersen (a fellow Scandinavian, whose unconventional writerly directness has echoes in his later compatriot) and Roald Dahl all open their own windows on to this world, arming us for the truth while they entertain.

Or, one last thought: perhaps it is child-friendly satire – a commentary on the idiocies of parents (whom Roald clearly identifies as the ultimate cause of the children's flaws) rather than politics?

Many commentators have pointed out the influence of *Alice's Adventures in Wonderland* and *Through the Looking-Glass* on *Charlie* in its setting (a world we recognize but which doesn't quite make sense), wordplay (buttergin, whipped cream, square sweets that look round) and slightly crazy, dream-like logic ('Nobody except squirrels can get walnuts whole out of walnut shells every time . . . But in my factory I insist upon using only whole walnuts. Therefore I have to have squirrels to do the job . . .'). But Carroll also subverted the conventions of his time. Alice was far more feisty a heroine than was customary – talking and fighting back against being made too big, too small or too decapitated at every turn – and most of the characters took their

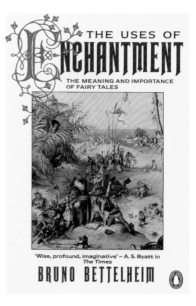

The Uses of Enchantment: The Meaning and Importance of Fairy Tales (Penguin, 1991).

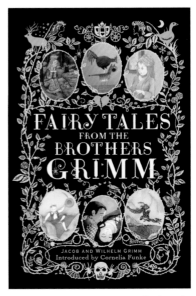

Fairy Tales from the Brothers Grimm (Puffin, 2012).

Illustrations by John Tenniel from
Alice's Adventures in Wonderland (1865).

inspiration from real life. The Lion and the Unicorn, as well as the Walrus and the Carpenter, were Disraeli and Gladstone respectively (with the oysters standing in for hapless voters), the two Queens and their two, very much overshadowed husbands versions of his own monarch Queen Victoria, and her consort Prince Albert, and the Caterpillar a take-off of a Victorian schoolmaster with his inane questions and pointless recitations. Carroll's child readers may not have got every reference, but their parents certainly would have, though librarians and critics seem not to damn him as they did Roald for straying into adult territory instead of staying on the child's level. Maybe time heals all wounds.

Certainly in the fifty years that have passed since *Charlie and the Chocolate Factory* was first published, the love for the book has only increased and the protests have receded. This must be, at least in part, because the book has now survived several reading generations. Parents today are the *Charlie* readers of yore, who were delighted, not corrupted, by Roald Dahl's darkness. And partly it is surely because greater threats to children's mental lives, liberties and happiness have subsumed those threats emanating from even the worst books. A modern fairy tale from the sixties, be it ever so discomfitingly unconventional, feels gently and quaintly edifying now –

Inside Charlie's Chocolate Factory

especially when set against gaming, social networking and the internet. At the click of a mouse, all these technological distractions make manifest worse nightmares than folklore could ever contemplate. So expands the canon.

Once the shock of this new sensibility erupting into the marketplace has worn off for all those involved, it becomes easier to locate and appreciate Roald's talents. First and foremost among these is his ability as a storyteller. There's no easy way to define this, no specific lines you can quote to prove it, any more than you can for the great storytellers in the world of adult books, from Anthony Trollope to John Grisham. It's a matter of keeping up a certain pace while still allowing yourself time to realize all the possibilities along the way, so that the reader keeps turning the page but never feels short-changed and can finish the book with a sigh of satisfaction rather than exasperation. I think that's the key to my own childhood love of *Charlie*. I went down each pink corridor with our hero (well yes, all right, in light of what I wrote before I suppose I can admit it – for the duration of the tale, I *was* that hero), I went round every room dazzled by the sights and sounds and smells, drawn on by the shimmering, gleeful, irresistible Mr Wonka, and pushed from behind by an author who knew exactly where we were going and how to get us there.

Inside Charlie's Chocolate Factory

Of course, children are not often bothered by the disapproval of grown-up critics. *Charlie and the Chocolate Factory* continues to entertain young (and old) readers around the world. In 2011, Puffin Books published a Draw Your Own Cover edition of *Charlie*, inviting readers to submit their creations. Here are just a few examples of how *Charlie* sparks children's imagination.

WhoWhatWhereWhenHow?

For fans of Roald Dahl, of course, one of the most common and irresistible habits – at least among those who make a habit of this sort of thing – is to try to map events and characters from the author's life on to his work. Sometimes a direct correlation is beyond doubt, and often explicitly confirmed by Roald in his autobiographical books *Boy* and *Going Solo* – like the caning in *Danny the Champion of the World*, which is clearly derived from his experiences of corporal punishment at school. His description of one in *Boy* is an almost word-for-word copy of that given in *Danny* – and in many interviews.

Roald Dahl himself cited his lifelong love of chocolate, beginning with the sweet shop in the village and the boxes of bars from Cadbury sent to the pupils of his boarding school to test, as the spark of inspiration for *Charlie*. The most tantalizing remaining question, of course, is: who is the real Willy Wonka?

The simplest, most obvious answer is that Willy Wonka is Roald Dahl. Both are eccentric, endlessly inventive, full of conviction – masters of their respective crafts of chocolate-making and storytelling. Both are fascinating, energetic men, never dull, full of humour, kindness and generosity – but who always keep you on your toes too. Roald's daughter Lucy tells the story of how when she and her siblings were young her father would tell them that dreams were mixed under a tree in the garden 'and then every night, rain or shine, he would go out and, with a bamboo pipe, blow dreams in through the window. For years we believed the Giant lived under one of the trees but we didn't dare ask which one in case we were thought stupid.' Doesn't that sound like just the kind of headspinning dual effect Willy Wonka in real life would have on you too? I always imagined that a conversation with either Roald Dahl or Willy Wonka would leave you feeling as exhausted and exhilarated as you would after swimming in a rough sea. And what is Roald, holed up in his writing hut ('It's good fun in there,' he once said. 'You live in that world, it's wonderful') but a man busy like Wonka in his factory, building his own glorious world within a world? Like the nonpareil chocolatier, with semi-magical conjuring of extraordinary confections that disapply the laws of physics, so did Roald let his imagination run riot, with millions of children across the globe loving him for it.

Less frivolously, it is impossible not to wonder how the loss of Olivia and Roald's experiences with Theo as he was writing and revising *Charlie* affected the book. Would there have been quite such fantastical excesses if Roald had not been seeking escape in his work from something so dreadful? Would there be quite such a pervasive sense in it that the children's safety cannot be guaranteed by anyone if the writer hadn't been someone who knew, inescapably, to his core, that this was so? Is the suggestion of darkness at the edges of the book, which so distinguished it from its contemporaries and continues to do so even amid today's harder-hitting competitors, a tiny measure of Roald's depthless grief at the time?

Theories of Criticism

These days Roald Dahl's books are almost a rite of passage for the young reader. Children discover them or are introduced to them (generally happily) by parents, teachers and librarians whose priorities are now, as Roald's always were, to get children reading.

Charlie is perhaps the most commercially successful of all Roald's books (though I can practically hear the thousands of *BFG*, *Witches*, *Twits* and *Matilda* fans getting ready to cry that it's had twenty years longer than most to become so). The tiny boy stepping out of his cold privation into the warm, wonderful world of Willy Wonka captures the hearts and minds of each generation anew. And – unlike Blyton, who becomes so unreadable once you are older that you look back on your child-self as someone utterly unrecognizable – it stands up to later re-reading. The charm, the galloping pace and the lonely boy finding his soulmate in a chimerical factory owner all remain as potent and intoxicating a treat as ever. Roald reaches out from the pages, hitches you up and pulls you inside the story as swiftly, confidently and thrillingly as ever. It's one giant whipple-scrumptious bar of delight and you stuff it down in delicious great chunks still.

Ultimately the secret of *Charlie*'s success and its enduring charm remains, like most secrets worth knowing, elusive. We wonder, imagine, apply this theory and that, but when we try to analyse *Charlie* – or indeed any book – it is probably best to always bear in mind the quote from Degas that Roald kept pinned up in his writing hut: 'Art is a lie to which one gives the accent of truth.' Or maybe to pin up in our own huts Roald's reply to an interviewer who once tried to analyse the deeper meanings of *Matilda* for him: 'Absolute tosh.'

So just go and read *Charlie* again – the one you remember from childhood. Not the one about a reader-substitute who embarks on an exercise in universal wish-fulfilment and resolves our socio-sexual-cultural anxieties and ambivalences along the way, but the one about the boy who wins a Golden Ticket and gets to visit an amazing chocolate factory run by a crazy man called Willy Wonka. It's a really good book.

THE MARXIST CRITICS

Marxism is the theory that the bourgeoisie (the boss class), who are the owners of the means of production (companies, machines, factories and so on, and the capital needed to set them up), exploit the proletariat (the under class: the people who actually make the stuff that the bosses go on to sell for profits that go into their, rather than the labourers', pockets), locking society in an eternal class struggle.

Karl Marx

So . . . you can see why it was always going to be difficult for Marxist critics to leave the story of a top-hatted factory owner getting rich off the back of a captive workforce labouring for literal beans alone, can't you?

According to Marxist theorists, the factory is the distilled essence of capitalism, with bourgeois Wonka exploiting the powerless labourers. First he fires all his employees for fear that spies have infiltrated the workplace (no mention of whether any of the non-spying ones take him to a tribunal and sue for unfair dismissal) and – in the ultimate demonstration of the replaceability of labour within the capitalist system which so weakens the working class's position, rendering them merely faceless factory fodder – seamlessly substitutes the Oompa-Loompas, who are so dependent on his support that they can be even more mercilessly exploited than the previous lot. They are not even paid in money but in cacao beans – which was surely illegal even before minimum-wage legislation was introduced. The uncomplaining Oompa-Loompas represent the false consciousness that pervades the working class, which makes them think of themselves as contented and unable to see that they are members of an oppressed class co-opted into supporting a system that only disadvantages them.

Nobody tell them about the elves in Santa's workshop, OK?

THE FREUDIANS

Freud believed that we have a subconscious mind and we lock up there all our deepest, darkest fears and desires. According to him, these include a fascination with bodily and sexual functions, secret longings to kill our fathers and marry our mothers, and tendencies towards masochism, sadism and other strange fetishes and fixations depending on when, where and how our various stages of childhood development became warped and by whom.

Sigmund Freud

Followers of Freud's teachings had a field day with *Charlie and the Chocolate Factory*. Which, by their lights, should be renamed *Charlie and the Great Digestive System* because their take on things is that:

1. The chocolate factory is symbolic of the human digestive tract – expelling the children it does not need at the other end like waste matter.

2. And it does all that when, of course, it is not busy symbolizing the unconscious mind, through which the ticket holders, representing various stages of childhood development, must pass before maturity is achieved.

Augustus Gloop is stuck at the early oral stage of psychosexual development. Never effectively weaned from Mrs Gloop, he is fixated on constant oral gratification and lies down to sup at the chocolate river – representative of the flow of a mother's milk.

Violet Beauregarde, on the other hand, has all the aggressive and sadistic tendencies of one who has moved on from sucking to chewing in the late oral stage of our unexpectedly complex journey through life/the chocolate factory. Her gum fetish is the manifestation of the desire for an external object that can permanently assuage the stress of hunger. Please treat the next packet you buy with the respect it deserves.

Inside Charlie's Chocolate Factory

Veruca Salt represents those conflicting desires of retention and release that denote the Freudians' second most famous gift to culture, psychology and comedy – the anal fixation. This stage is further characterized by possessiveness ('I want . . . I want . . . !') and sadism.

Now, what on earth is there left for violence-loving, gun-toting *Mike Teavee* to represent? Yes, that's right – the phallic stage! This is, of course, the stage in childhood when we first begin to recognize our genitals as a source of physical pleasure, and generally coincides with the onset of the Oedipal stage (Mike presumably has come to the Wonka factory with his mother because he killed his father before they left home).

Or:
Each of the children had bad experiences during potty training, causing them to obsess over the nearest symbolic replacement for the faeces they were 'losing'. Augustus is trying to replace with food the vital innards that he believed were falling out of his bottom, Veruca now hates losing anything at all and keeps trying to gather everything she sees to her, Violet was given a dummy to soothe her during stressful potty times, and some primeval part of Mike's brain only conceives that his parents tried to distract him with TV to prevent him realizing that a little bit of himself was being flushed down the loo.

The children's unhappy fates encourage child readers to move on through their own adolescence or pre-adolescence and not become sad cases of arrested development, forever stuck in choco-neural tubes of immaturity.

As for Willy Wonka (I'll leave it to you to figure out what the Freudians make of his name), he's suffering from castration anxiety. He is stuck in the latency period that attends the fear of losing what is most important to a man: here represented by the chocolate recipes the spies tried to steal from Wonka, prompting him to lock himself up in a towering factory and protect himself from further threats or damage.

Overall, according to Freudian critic Hamida Bosmajian, *Charlie and the Chocolate Factory* 'allows children to indulge . . . amorally in [a] liberating and libidinal satiric fantasy . . . and releases a child's anxieties about bodily functions, physical injury and death'.

So. Now you know. I'd like to blame this all on the sixties, but alas it's still going on.

'Nothing is impossible'

Reading is not simple. Children are not simple. Together, they are even more complicated than the sum of their parts. As most of us will well remember, we liked to feel thrilled and excited, we liked our characters – even and especially the ones we identify with – to be imperilled, but we also – crucially – liked to feel safe. Encompassing both desires and exploiting the tension between them is something Roald does better than anyone. Someone once said that the art of jazz is knowing how far out you can go and still get back in. Reading Roald Dahl is like that. He takes his readers on adventures full of thrills and spills, he will throw in handfuls of unexpected twists and turns, but you know he will get you back safely. He will push at your boundaries, make your child-brain boggle but still get you – breathless, laughing, exhilarated – home again.

Charlie and Grandpa Joe come home, illustrated by Quentin Blake.

Inside Charlie's Chocolate Factory

Acknowledgements

Thank you to the following people who were kind enough to grant me interviews for this book: John August, Quentin Blake, Michael Böllner, Catherine Butler, Theo Dahl, Julie Dawn Cole, Michael Foreman, David Greig, Matthew Hardy, Freddie Highmore, Douglas Hodge, Nicholas Logsdail, Alex McDowell, Caro Newling, Denise Nickerson, Sheila St Lawrence and Mark Thompson.

And thank you especially: to Julie Dawn Cole and Donald Sturrock for their further help in locating other people and items of interest; to the Roald Dahl Museum and Story Centre; to the Seven Stories National Centre for Children's Books; to Random House for allowing the use of the Joseph Schindelman interview from their archives; and to Luke Kelly and the Dahl estate for all their support.

Writing this book has been a pleasure and an honour.

Bibliography

Bettelheim, Bruno, *The Uses of Enchantment: The Meaning and Importance of Fairy Tales* (Penguin, 1991)

Bosmajian, Hamida, '*Charlie and the Chocolate Factory* and Other Excremental Visions', *The Lion and the Unicorn*, Vol. 9 (1985), pp. 36–49

Bradford, Clare, 'Chapter 4: Race, Ethnicity and Colonialism', in David Rudd, ed., *The Routledge Companion to Children's Literature* (Routledge, 2010), pp.39–50

Brenner, Max, *Chocolate: A Love Story: 65 Chocolate Recipes from Max Brenner's Private Collection* (Little Brown US, 2009)

Burton, Tim, *Burton on Burton* (Faber & Faber, 2006)

Cameron, Eleanor, 'McLuhan, Youth and Literature', *Horn Book Magazine*, Parts I–III (October 1972–April 1973) (including '*Charlie and the Chocolate Factory*: A Reply' in February 1973 and 'A Reply to Roald Dahl' in April 1973)

Cartmell, Deborah, 'Section 4: Screen Classics', in Janet Maybin and Nicola J. Watson, ed., *Children's Literature: Approaches and Territories* (Palgrave Macmillan, The Open University, 2009), pp. 281–295

Cole, Julie Dawn, *I Want it Now! A Memoir of Life on the Set of Willy Wonka and the Chocolate Factory* (BearManor Media/ Ocean View Publishing, 2011)

Dahl, Roald, *Boy: Tales of Childhood* (Puffin, 2013 edition; first published in Great Britain by Jonathan Cape Ltd and in the USA by Farrar, Straus and Giroux, 1984)

—, *Charlie and the Chocolate Factory* (various editions; first published in the USA by Knopf, 1964; published in Great Britain by Allen & Unwin, 1967; published by Puffin Books, 1973)

—, *Charlie and the Great Glass Elevator* (Puffin, 1975; first published in the USA by Knopf, 1972; published in Great Britain by Allen & Unwin, 1973)

—, *Going Solo* (Puffin, 2013 edition; first published in Great Britain by Jonathan Cape Ltd and in the USA by Farrar, Straus and Giroux, 1986)

—, *Matilda* (Puffin, 1989; first published in Great Britain by Jonathan Cape Ltd, 1988)

Dahl, Roald, and Liccy, *Memories with Food at Gipsy House* (Viking, 1991); republished as *Roald Dahl's Cookbook* (Penguin, 1996)

Head, Steve, 'Scott Frank's Adventures with *Charlie and the Chocolate Factory*', *IGN* [website] (15 September 2001) <http://uk.ign.com/articles/2001/09/15/scott-franks-adventures-with-charlie-and-the-chocolate- factory>

Hollindale, Peter, '"And Children Swarmed to Him Like Settlers, He Became a Land." The Outrageous Success of Roald Dahl', in Julia Briggs, Dennis Butts and M. O. Grenby, ed., *Popular Children's Literature in Britain* (Ashgate, 2008), pp. 271–286

Lauren, Dylan, *Dylan's Candy Bar: Unwrap Your Sweet Life* (Clarkson Potter, 2010)

Lurie, Alison, *Don't Tell the Grown-Ups* (Bloomsbury, 1990)

Martin, Douglas, 'Chapter 3: Faith Jaques' and 'Chapter 16: Michael Foreman', *The Telling Line: Essays on Fifteen Contemporary Book Illustrators* (Walker Books, 1989), pp.60–82, 291–308

McKee, Victoria, 'You gotta roll with it' [about the making of the film adaptation of *James and the Giant Peach*, with reference to the conversation between Liccy Dahl and Tim Burton on page 65], *Independent* (26 July 1996)

Stuart, Mel, and Josh Young, *Pure Imagination: The Making of Willy Wonka and the Chocolate Factory* (St Martin's Press, 2002)

Sturrock, Donald, *Storyteller: The Life of Roald Dahl* (HarperCollins, 2010)

Tatar, Maria, *Enchanted Hunters: the Power of Stories in Childhood* (W. W. Norton & Company, 2009)

Treglown, Jeremy, *Roald Dahl* (Faber & Faber, 1994)

Townsend, John Rowe, *Written for Children* (Bodley Head, 1990)

Toynbee, Polly, 'Mystery Man: Behind the Lines', *Guardian* (23 December 1985)

West, Mark, 'Interview with Roald Dahl', *Children's Literature in Education*, Vol. 21, No.2 (1990), pp.65–66

Wilder, Gene, *Kiss Me Like a Stranger: My Search for Love and Art* (St Martin's Press, 2005)

Wolper, David, with David Fisher, *Producer: A Memoir* (Scribner, 2003)

Alston, Ann, and Catherine Butler, ed., *Roald Dahl: A Collection of All New Critical Essays* (Palgrave Macmillan, 2012)

Discography

B-Baz, 'Willy Wonka, Willy Wonka (Interlude)', *Genesis* (2012)

Khalifa, Wiz, 'Purple Flowers', *Yellow Starships* (2012)

West, Kanye, 'Monster', *My Beautiful Dark Twisted Fantasy* (2010)

Filmography

Charlie and the Chocolate Factory, directed by Tim Burton (Warner Bros, 2005)

'Pure Imagination: *The Story of Willy Wonka and the Chocolate Factory*' documentary [includes an interview with David Seltzer, quoted on page 74], in *Willy Wonka and the Chocolate Factory: 40th Anniversary Ultimate Collector's Edition* (Warner Bros, 2011)

Willy Wonka and the Chocolate Factory, directed by Mel Stuart (Paramount/ Warner Bros, 1971)

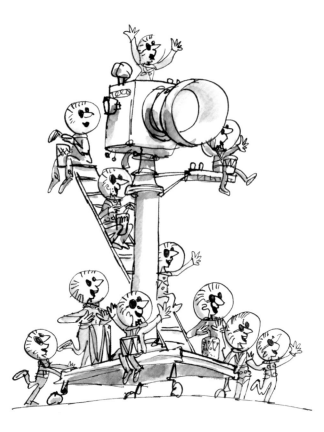

Picture Credits

Every effort has been made to trace copyright holders and to obtain their permission for the use of copyright material. The publisher apologizes for any errors or omissions and would be grateful if notified of any corrections that should be incorporated in future reprints or editions of this book.

Photograph of Sophie Dahl courtesy of Sophie Dahl. Photograph of Lucy Mangan courtesy of *Stylist* magazine.

Covers of Knopf editions are reproduced by kind permission of Alfred A. Knopf, an imprint of Random House Children's Books, a division of Random House LLC.

The illustrations by Quentin Blake and Michael Foreman are used by kind permission of the respective artists. The illustrations by Faith Jaques are used by kind permission of the Family of Faith Jaques. Illustrations by Joseph Schindelman, copyright © 1964, renewed 1992 by Joseph Schindelman; from *Charlie and the Chocolate Factory* by Roald Dahl. Used by permission of Alfred A. Knopf, an imprint of Random House Children's Books, a division of Random House LLC. All rights reserved. Any third-party use of this material, outside of this publication, is prohibited. Interested parties must apply directly to Random House LLC for permission.

Elements from the motion pictures *Willy Wonka and the Chocolate Factory* (1971) and *Charlie and the Chocolate Factory* (2005) used courtesy of Warner Bros Entertainment Inc. All elements are ™ and copyright © Warner Bros Entertainment, Inc.

SUGAR-COATED PENCILS: Writing the Book

Page 1: Roald Dahl photograph copyright © Nick Nicolson. Courtesy of the Roald Dahl Museum and Story Centre.

Page 5: Dahl family photograph copyright © George Konig. Courtesy of the Roald Dahl Museum and Story Centre.

Pages 8, 11, 13, 14, 16–17 and 30 images copyright © Roald Dahl Nominee Ltd. Courtesy of the Roald Dahl Museum and Story Centre.

Page 33: [Oompa-Loompas] AF archive/Alamy.

TELEVISION CHOCOLATE: On Stage and Screen

Pages 36–37: [1971 film poster] Warner Bros/The Kobal Collection.

Page 38: [1971 DVD cover] REX/Moviestore Collection.

Page 39: [2005 film poster] REX/c.Warner Br/Everett; [2013 musical poster] London Stage Musical Production, 2014; poster for Opera Theatre of Saint Louis copyright © TOKY, 2010 (toky.com).

Page 40: [1971 film poster] REX/Courtesy Everett Collection.

Page 41: [Mel Stuart and Oompa-Loompa actors] Wolper/Warner Bros/The Kobal Collection; [Gene Wilder and child actors] Dan Callister/Alamy.

Page 43: [Gene Wilder and the Oompa-Loompa actors] Wolper/Warner Bros/The Kobal Collection; [Michael Böllner, Günter Meisner and Ursula Reit] REX/Everett Collection.

Page 44: [Julie Dawn Cole] Wolper/Warner Bros/The Kobal Collection; [Denise Nickerson as Violet Beauregarde] DDP/Camera Press.

Page 45: [Paris Themmen] Dan Callister/Alamy; [Peter Ostrum] Wolper/Warner Bros/The Kobal Collection.

Page 46: [Joel Grey] REX/c.Everett Collection; [Fred Astaire] Paul W. Bailey/NBC/NBCU Photo Bank via Getty Images.

Page 47: [Gene Wilder] Wolper/Warner Bros/The Kobal Collection.

Page 49: [Gene Wilder in his Willy Wonka outfit] Wolper/Warner Bros/The Kobal Collection.

Pages 50–51: Wolper/Warner Bros/The Kobal Collection; except page 51 (left – 'Inventing Room') Photo12/DR.

Page 52: [David Seltzer] REX/c.20thC.Fox/Everett.

Page 53: [Entering the Chocolate Room] Wolper/Warner Bros/The Kobal Collection.

Page 54: [Peter Ostrum as Charlie] REX/Everett Collection; [Julie Dawn Cole] Steve Schapiro/Corbis.

Pages 55–57: [The Golden Egg room, Augustus Gloop and Violet Beauregarde] Wolper/Warner Bros/The Kobal Collection.

Page 58: [Wonka's 'half' office] Wolper/Warner Bros/The Kobal Collection; [Great Glass Elevator] Photo12/DR.

Page 59: [1971 film, French poster] Wolper/Warner Bros; illustration copyright © Barbara Baranowska; image courtesy of Daniel Bird.

Page 60 (left): [Charlie looking in shop window] Wolper/Warner Bros/The Kobal Collection.

Page 60 (right): [Oompa-Loompa] REX/Everett Collection.

Pages 60–61 (centre image): [Willy Wonka] Wolper/Warner Bros/The Kobal Collection.

Page 61: [Willy Wonka] AF archive/Alamy; [Charlie] Photos 12/Alamy.

Page 62: [Rusty Goffe] REX/Startraks Photo; [Rusty Goffe inset] Wolper/Warner Bros/The Kobal Collection; [Peter Ostrum] REX/ITV; [Peter Ostrum inset] REX/Everett Collection; [Michael Böllner] REX/ITV; [Michael Böllner inset] Dan Callister/Alamy.

Page 63: [Denise Nickerson] REX/ITV; [Denise Nickerson inset] Dan Callister/Alamy; [Paris Themmen] REX/Startraks Photo; [Paris Themmen inset] Dan Callister/Alamy; [Julie Dawn Cole] REX/ITV; [Julie Dawn Cole inset] Wolper/Warner Bros/The Kobal Collection; [Gene Wilder] Kim Komenich/San Francisco Chronicle/Corbis; [Gene Wilder inset] Wolper/Warner Bros/The Kobal Collection.

Page 64: [2005 film poster] REX/Moviestore Collection.

Page 65: [*Danny the Champion of the World*] DDP/Camera Press; [*James and the Giant Peach* poster] REX/Courtesy Everett Collection, copyright © Walt Disney.

Page 66: Postcard from Roald Dahl reproduced by kind permission of John August.

Page 67: [Johnny Depp with Tim Burton] REX/c.Warner Br/Everett; [Deep Roy as the Oompa-Loompas] Warner Bros/The Kobal Collection; [Freddie Highmore as Charlie] Warner Bros/The Kobal Collection/Peter Mountain.

Pages 68–69 (top row): [first, third and fourth film images] Warner Bros/The Kobal Collection/Peter Mountain; [second and fifth film images] Warner Bros/The Kobal Collection.

Pages 68–69 (bottom row): [first, second and fourth film images] Warner Bros/The Kobal Collection; [third and fifth film images] Warner Bros/The Kobal Collection/Peter Mountain.

Page 70: [The chocolate river (2005)] Warner Bros/The Kobal Collection/Peter Mountain.

Page 71: [Wonka's boat (2005)] Warner Bros/The Kobal Collection.

Pages 72–73: Tim Burton sketchbooks copyright © Tim Burton, 2004. All rights reserved. Courtesy of Warner Bros. Entertainment Inc.

Page 75: [Posters] Moviestore collection Ltd/Alamy.

Pages 79 and 79: [Johnny Depp as Willy Wonka] REX/c.Warner Br/Everett.

Page 78: [Gene Wilder as Willy Wonka] Wolper/Warner Bros/The Kobal Collection.

Page 80: [Charlie and the Bucket family – close-up] Warner Bros/The Kobal Collection; [Charlie and the Bucket family – group image] Warner Bros/The Kobal Collection/Peter Mountain.

Pages 82–83: [film image (2005)] Warner Bros/The Kobal Collection/Peter Mountain.

Page 84: Douglas Hodge photograph copyright © Helen Maybanks. Reproduced by kind permission of Playful Productions/Cornershop PR.

Page 85: [Sam Mendes] Dave M. Benett/Getty Images.

Page 86: *Charlie and the Chocolate Factory: The Musical* (Wonka factory gates) photograph copyright © Brinkhoff/Moegenburg. Reproduced by kind permission of Playful Productions/Cornershop PR.

Pages 87–88: *Charlie and the Chocolate Factory: The Musical* photographs copyright © Helen Maybanks; except page 88 (bottom image) Charlie at the rubbish dump photograph copyright © Brinkhoff/Moegenburg. All photographs reproduced by kind permission of Playful Productions/Cornershop PR.

Pages 89–93: *The Golden Ticket* photographs copyright © Ken Howard/Opera Theatre of Saint Louis.

Page 94: *Charlie and the Chocolate Factory* brochure photograph by Mandy Norman; copyright © Penguin Books Ltd, 2014.

Page 97: Costume design sketches for *The Golden Ticket* by Martin Pakledinaz. Copyright © Martin Pakledinaz, 2010. Used by permission of the Family of Martin Pakledinaz.

BEHIND THE GATES OF THE CHOCOLATE FACTORY: A Visual Tour

Page 101: Joseph Schindelman photograph courtesy of Random House US.

Page 102: Faith Jaques photograph used by permission of the Family of Faith Jaques. Courtesy of Seven Stories – National Centre for Children's Books.

Page 103: Michael Foreman photograph copyright © Ron Sutherland. Reproduced by kind permission of Michael Foreman.

Pages 104–105: Photographs courtesy of Quentin Blake.

Page 120: Tim Burton's sketch copyright © Tim Burton, 2004. All rights reserved. Courtesy of Warner Bros Entertainment, Inc.

Pages 120–121:[The Oompa-Loompas (2005)] Warner Bros/The Kobal Collection.

Page 122: [The SS *Wonkatania*] Warner Bros/Allstar.

Page 124: [The Inventing Room (1971)] Wolper/Warner Bros/The Kobal Collection.

Page 125: [The Inventing Room (2005)] REX/Moviestore Collection.

Pages 128 and 131: [The Nut Room (2005) and Television-Chocolate Room (2005)] Warner Bros/The Kobal Collection/Peter Mountain.

Page 131: [The Television-Chocolate Room (1971)] REX/Everett Collection.

Page 133: [The Great Glass Elevator (2005)] Warner Bros/The Kobal Collection.

EVERLASTING GOBSTOPPERS: The Effect on Popular Culture

Pages 134–135: Photograph by Mandy Norman; copyright © Penguin Books Ltd, 2014. (The Kubrick™ figurines are based on *Charlie and the Chocolate Factory* (2005 film) ™ and copyright © Warner Bros. Entertainment Inc.)

Page 136: Photograph by Mandy Norman; copyright © Penguin Books Ltd, 2014. LEGO® creation by Nick Franklin.

Page 137: *Gobstopper* image copyright © Funny or Die Inc., 2009. All rights reserved. Part of the Turner Entertainment Digital Network.

Page 138: [Russell Brand] Scott Heavey/Getty Images.

Page 139: Photographs courtesy of Charlie and the Chocolate Factory™: The Ride, at Alton Towers Resort.

Page 140: Photographs by Mandy Norman; copyright © Penguin Books Ltd, 2014.

Page 141: Photographs by Mandy Norman; copyright © Penguin Books Ltd, 2014. (The Kubrick™ figurines and Pullip doll are based on *Charlie and the Chocolate Factory* (2005 film) ™ and copyright © Warner Bros. Entertainment Inc.)

Page 142: Golden Record LP copyright © Golden Records/Verse Music Group.

Page 143: [*Saturday Night Live* (2002 and 2011)] Dana Edelson/NBC/NBCU Photo Bank via Getty Images.

Page 144: [*Epic Movie* (2007)] 20th Century Fox/The Kobal Collection/John P Johnson; [*30 Rock*] Ali Goldstein/NBC/NBCU Photo Bank via Getty Images.

Page 147: Gameboy Advance (2005) and PlayStation 2 (2005) video games reproduced by kind permission of Warner Bros. Entertainment Inc.

Page 148: [Veruca Salt] Frank Mullen/WireImage/Getty Images.

Page 149: Matthew Hardy with Julie Dawn Cole photograph copyright © James Penlidis. Reproduced by kind permission of Matthew Hardy.

Page 150: Matthew Hardy poster artwork copyright © Joe White. Reproduced by kind permission of Matthew Hardy.

Page 152: [Willy Wonka meme] makeameme.org; [Charlie and Veruca Salt memes] quickmeme.com; [Grandpa Joe meme] imgur.com.

Page 153: [*Just Desserts*] Trae Patton/Bravo/NBCU Photo Bank via Getty Images.

Pages 154–155: Lauren Dylan and Dylan's Candy Bar photographs copyright © Dylan's Candy Bar.

Page 156: [Jacques Torres] Cindy Ord/Getty Images.

WHIPPLE-SCRUMPTIOUS FUDGEMALLOW DELIGHT: All About Chocolate

Pages 158–159: Wonka Bar branding reproduced by kind permission of Nestlé.

Pages 160–162: Wonka chocolate promotions and trade brochure (1970s) photographs courtesy of Dan Goodsell.

Page 164: Wonka products reproduced by kind permission of Nestlé.

Page 165: [top left] Spencer Platt/Getty Images; [top right] reproduced by kind permission of Nestlé; [bottom middle and left] photographs courtesy of Dan Goodsell; [bottom right] razorpix/Alamy.

Page 168: Sweet! Hollywood store photographs reproduced by kind permission of Nestlé.

Page 169: Wonka products reproduced by kind permission of Nestlé.

Pages 170–71: Cadbury's chocolate packaging (various) reproduced by kind permission of Cadbury.

Page 173: Foil-wrapper ball photograph copyright © Roald Dahl Nominee Ltd, courtesy of the Roald Dahl Museum and Story Centre; botanical drawings copyright © Penguin Books Ltd, 2014.

Page 174: [George Cadbury] Whitlock/Spencer Arnold/Hulton Archive/Getty Images; [John Cadbury and his family] Mary Evans Picture Library/John Maclellan.

Page 175: [Rowntrees photographs] Nestlé/BNPS.co.uk.

Page 176: Red box photograph copyright © Penguin Books Ltd, 2014.

Page 177: [Mars chocolate bar advertisement] Mary Evans/Retrograph Collection.

Page 178: Smarties advertisement reproduced by kind permission of Nestlé.

Page 179: [After Eight and KitKat adverts, and Aero window display] Nestlé/BNPS.co.uk; [1950s magazine advert] Jeff Morgan 12/Alamy.

SQUARE SWEETS THAT LOOK ROUND: What the Critics and Fans Say

Page 182: Roald Dahl photograph copyright © Roald Dahl Nominee Ltd. Courtesy of the Roald Dahl Museum and Story Centre.

Page 184: [Augustus Gloop (2005)] REX/Moviestore Collection.

Page 185: Reprinted from the October 1972 issue of the *Horn Book Magazine* by permission of The Horn Book, Inc., www.hbook.com.

Page 187: Roald and Theo Dahl photograph courtesy of the Roald Dahl Museum and Story Centre.

Page 201: [Karl Marx] Private Collection/The Bridgeman Art Library.

Page 202: [Sigmund Freud] RA/Lebrecht Music & Arts.

Index

Fictional characters are indexed under their first names. Page references for images are in italics.

THERE'S MORE TO

ROALD DAHL

THAN GREAT STORIES ...

Did you know that **10%** of Roald Dahl's royalties*
go to help the work of the Roald Dahl charities?

Roald Dahl is famous for his stories and rhymes, but much less well known is how often he went out of his way to help seriously ill children. Today **Roald Dahl's Marvellous Children's Charity** helps children with the severest conditions and the greatest needs. The charity believes every child can have a more marvellous life, no matter how ill they are, or how short their life may be.

Can you do something marvellous to help others?
Find out how at **www.roalddahlcharity.org**

You can find out about Roald Dahl's real-life experiences and how they found their way into his stories at the **Roald Dahl Museum and Story Centre** in Great Missenden, Buckinghamshire (the author's home village). The Museum is a charity that aims to inspire excitement about reading, writing and creativity. There are three fun and fact-packed galleries, with lots to make, do and see (including Roald Dahl's writing hut). Aimed at 6–12-year-olds, the Museum is open to the public and to school groups throughout the year.

Find out more at **www.roalddahlmuseum.org**

Roald Dahl's Marvellous Children's Charity (RDMCC) is a registered charity no. 1137409.
The Roald Dahl Museum and Story Centre (RDMSC) is a registered charity no. 1085853.
The Roald Dahl Charitable Trust is a registered charity no. 1119330 and supports the work of RDMCC and RDMSC.
* Donated royalties are net of commission